BIBLICAL WORLDVIEW ANI

CHRISTIANITY *in* BUSINESS

Applying Biblical Values in the Marketplace

ERNEST P. LIANG

EDITOR

THE CENTER FOR CHRISTIANITY IN BUSINESS

HOUSTON BAPTIST UNIVERSITY

HIGH BRIDGE BOOKS

HOUSTON

Christianity in Business
Edited by Ernest P. Liang

Center for Christianity in Business, Archie W. Dunham College of Business, Houston Baptist University, 7502 Fondren Road, Houston, Texas 77074.

Printed in the United States of America
ISBN (Paperback): 978-1-946615-81-7
ISBN (e-book): 978-1-946615-26-8

High Bridge Books titles may be purchased in bulk for educational, business, fundraising, or sales promotional use. For information, please contact High Bridge Books via www.HighBridgeBooks.com/contact.

Published in Houston, Texas by High Bridge Books

This book is dedicated to all Christ followers who desire to walk closer with God and answer His call to be salt and light as they navigate the torrents of the modern world of business affairs.

About the HBU Center for Christianity in Business

The Center for Christianity in Business is a marketplace outreach ministry of the Archie W. Dunham College of Business at Houston Baptist University in Houston, Texas, USA. It is dedicated to challenging and equipping present and future Christian business leaders to integrate biblical values and principles in their personal and professional lives. The Center offers valuable resources to afford marketplace professionals lifelong learning opportunities in faith-work integration. The ministry is based on the vision that ALL Christian business leaders and professionals can serve as ministers of God's Church so that they can become "the salt and light of the world" (Matt. 5:13-16). For more information visit www.hbu.edu/ccb.

The Biblical Worldview and the Marketplace Series will be devoted to monographs that provide original, inspiring insights into the practical application of biblical principles in the conduct of business affairs. Manuscript proposals are welcome. Send an inquiry to ccb@hbu.edu.

Contents

INTRODUCTION

There is not a square inch in the whole domain of our human existence over which Christ, who is Sovereign over all, does not cry: "Mine!"

—ABRAHAM KUYPER

THIS IS NOT JUST A BOOK FOR Christian professionals active in the marketplace. This is a book for all Christians who interact with the world of commerce, and that practically means every believer. From the full-time housewife who is engaged in what economists called non-market production, to the retiree who steers his or her savings wagon through the maze of financial instruments intermediated by financial professionals and institutions, the marketplace is an integral part of our daily life. God intends believers to glorify Him in everything we do (1 Cor. 10:31), and that includes our activities—regardless of our roles—in the business world. This book purports to enlighten the rules of our commercial engagement with biblical principles, so that believers can be better, more effective stewards in God's economy. This indeed is the mission and purpose of this new series of publications from HBU's Center for Christianity in Business, of which this book is the inaugural title.

Beyond acting as God's helper in promoting human flourishing with our production and, yes, consumption, activities, the Christian business professional has also been called by God to be "salt and light" in this fallen world (Matt. 5:13-14). As born-again followers of Jesus, Christians are the "salt" that triumphs over the decay and the "light" that pierces the darkness in the world. In order to live out this God-given purpose, we as followers of Christ must unite biblical principles with business practices. As we do this, we will help to fulfill three imperatives in God's will for the world of commerce: spiritual, moral, and economic.

Spiritual

Christian business professionals often have a sharp sacred-secular divide that severely limits their usefulness for Christian service in the marketplace. Yet Christians ought to believe that business itself is a spiritual journey and a holy service to God.[1] Jesus urges followers to "Let your light shine before men in such a way that they may see your good works and glorify your father who is in heaven" (Matt. 5:14). In other words, the marketplace must be the Christian's mission field. Doing "good work"—work that glorifies God and reflects His lovingkindness—is how Christians redeem the marketplace from the corruption of a fallen world. Our work becomes an act of worship, and God is glorified in the making of money.

Paul admonishes Christians to "continue to work out your salvation..., for it is God who works in you to will and to act according to his purpose" (Phil. 2:12–13). For Christian business professionals, the marketplace is where God does most of the shaping of our character. It is where our Christian faith, through testing and endurance, becomes mature. If we will allow God to take charge of our work life, through His Holy Spirit, He will cause us to grow in godly character (Ezek. 36:27).

Not only does business allow us to minister to our fellow man, but it allows us to exercise our God-given creativity. God, the Creator, was the first to work in the material world. We are nearest to God and most like Him when we produce good things for the advance of human flourishing. It's in the world of business that we find some of the best opportunities to express this creative ability. It's also in the world of business that our stewardship of God's creation, from our own endowed ability, to people and things that undergird networks of relationships, is given meaningful practice and training. The world of commerce is a big incubator of spiritual maturity.

Moral

The participation of the Christian in the sphere of commerce carries an intrinsic moral connotation. As Richard Niebuhr observed, "The Christian must carry on cultural work in obedience to the Lord" because all of culture is under the judgment of God, and yet culture is also under God's sovereign rule.[2] What is "moral" and socially ethical in the context of our involvement in the marketplace must be informed by Scripture and defined by the will, word, and work of God. As a matter of strategy, the objective of Christian social ethics is to facilitate social reforms that will bring culture, and in this case, the marketplace, into closer conformity with what is just, good, and right.[3]

It is in the handling of things that we, as Christ followers, have the greatest opportunity to develop our moral nature as God's image-bearers. Absent the complex, sometimes treacherous nature of business relations, which are often governed by opportunistic behaviors engendered by information asymmetry, human passions and depravity, Christians would deprive themselves of vital opportunities to develop such Christian virtues as goodwill, integrity, patience, generosity, compassion, and faithfulness. Economists have often described the firm as nothing more than a "nexus of contracts"—contracts that carry inherent moral contents.[4] Whether the fallen world of commerce can be redeemed for the glory of God depends on the benevolent stewarding of relationships and the integrity of their moral (biblically informed) underpinnings.

The exercise of our God-endowed moral sentiment is tightly coupled with the advancement of human flourishing and our happiness. Adam Smith acknowledged this much when he wrote,

> ...the happiness of mankind...seems to have been the original purpose intended by [the Creator]....No other end seems worthy of that supreme wisdom and divine benignity which we necessarily ascribe to him...By acting according to our moral faculties we necessarily pursue the most effectual means for promoting the happiness of mankind...to cooperate with the Deity, and to advance as far as in our power the plan of Providence.[5]

Economic

Theologian Carl Henry concluded some time ago that "all schemes of economic recovery which isolate economic thought and behavior from the spiritual and moral world cannot secure human wellbeing, because economic activity which is not in the service of God gravitates to the service of the demonic... Separate the economic sphere from the living God and His claims, and men will drift from one crisis to another under any economic formula."[6]

It is true that in the marketplace, participants are all constrained by the rules of justice, established through a system of laws and institutions charged with enforcing those laws. This system helps to incentivize compliance with those rules, reduce risk, and promote trust, which is essential for capital exchange and growth. As Adam Smith would admit, the constraints of civic ethics and positive laws are the only barriers that stand between one's wealth and its loss to unconstrained greed.[7]

Sadly, in an ever-expanding commercial market system populated by free, enterprising individuals, government alone cannot provide this necessary constraint. In the absence of absolutist moral codes, the expansion of government policing necessary to enforce appropriate constraints would turn that free market into a police state. The subsequent repression of freedom would cripple creative and dynamic commerce. It is only when individuals obey moral codes that government can properly constrain the unethical few. Not only does this preserve the free market, but it prevents the government from falling prey to its own unconstrained greed—either for the money or the power entrusted to the institution.

The marketplace is populated by fallen individuals, who easily succumb to opportunistic and unethical desires if there are no (or inadequate) outward behavioral constraints. The frailty of fallen humanity cannot stand against the "animal spirit"—the "fleshly passions" (Rom. 7:5) as the Apostle Paul readily points out. As fallen beings, we don't desire good (Gal. 5:19–21) and we are unable to obey God's law (Rom. 8:3). Adam Smith's "Invisible hand," under which the economic system (or the marketplace) would prosper, is grounded in his faith in the working of a natural moral code inherent in economic agents. Smith's deistic faith in "the providential care of (God), His wisdom and goodness, even in the weakness and folly of man" provides the hope for his moral vision. We must work within a system that requires us, according to Adam Smith, to act in "accordance to our moral faculties."[8] Scripture tells us Christ offers us a new self, created in righteousness and holiness of the truth (Eph. 4:22-24). Smith's faith in the natural moral code undergirding the invisible hand is naturally fulfilled in Christ followers who live to please God.

This makes the Christian an invaluable economic asset in the world of business. If Christians are to obey God's call to be "salt and light," they can provide a stabilizing force in a turbulent and frenzied marketplace, not only by setting a righteous example in their actions but by shifting the focus from the temporal to the eternal. Christians act as "salt" by adhering to their biblical moral constraints and by holding others accountable. They act as "light" by living out this moral persuasion in their relationships and dealings. By adhering to faithful stewardship,

Christians facilitate economic prosperity and human flourishing while helping to redeem business for the Kingdom of God.

About this book

This book is a collection of essays, first published in the *Christian Business Review* journal, that center on stewardship and the biblical foundations of leading business enterprises. It represents a diversity of perspectives on an immense subject offered by some of the leading experts (academics and practitioners) in integrating the Christian faith in the practice of modern business. It offers a starting point for cultivating a worldview that will enable readers to apply biblical principles and values as they engage the marketplace. Any serious follower of Christ would desire to respond positively to Jesus' call to be "salt and light" in our sojourn through this fallen world, and we pray that this book will offer a window into the why and how Christians can fulfill this calling and help redeem the world of commerce for the glory of God and His Kingdom.

Ernest P. Liang, PhD
Editor
Houston, Texas

Notes

[1] Guy Morrill, *You and Yours* (New York: Fleming Revell Co., 1922). Accessed digital version at *http://books.google.com*.

[2] Richard Niebuhr, *Christ and Culture* (New York: Harper & Row, 1951), 191.

[3] David W. Gill, "Social Ethics" in *Evangelical Dictionary of Theology*, ed. Walter Elwell (Grand Rapids, MI.: Baker Books, 1984), 1023-27.

[4] Michael Jensen & William H. Meckling, "The Theory of the Firm: Managerial Behavior, Agency Costs, and Ownership Structure," *Journal of Financial Economics* (3(4), 1976), 305-360.

[5] Adam Smith, *The Theory of Moral Sentiments*, ed. D.D. Raphael and A.L. Macfie, Vol. 1 of D.D. Raphael and Andrew Skinner, eds.., *The Glasgow Edition of the Works and Correspondence of Adam Smith*, Oxford: Clarendon Press, (1976), 165-66.

[6] Carl Henry, "Christianity and the Economic Crisis," in *Vital Speeches of the Day*, (21(15), 1955), 1244. Retrieved from Military and Government Collection Database.

[7] Jerry Evensky, "Adam Smith's Essentials: On Trust, Faith, and Free Markets," *Journal of the History of Economic Thought* (33(2), 2011), 249-67.

[8] Ibid.

1

The First Word on Business

By David W. Gill & Al Erisman

WHAT ARE THE TOP TEN ethical issues and challenges facing Christian business people today? Answers: honesty, corruption and bribery, fair wages for workers, executive compensation, debt, product quality, sales tactics, unfair hiring and promotion practices, dangerous or unhealthy products or services, employee gossip… you can imagine the list.

Now, what would God's answers be? Would his list look like ours? The point is that God already has written the list: the Ten Commandments. On God's list, the first issue is always *who* is going to be God here? The text makes this plain:

> I am the Lord your God, who brought you out of Egypt, the land of slavery. You shall have no other gods before me. (Exodus 20:2-3)

The reach of this command goes far beyond business, of course. In every arena of life, having the true God on the throne is *the* decisive question, the point of departure.

The first commandment is stated as a simple, straightforward prohibition: "You shall have no other gods before me" (Exod. 20:3; Deut. 5:7). Jewish tradition views this as the *second* "word," with the earlier statement, "I am the Lord your God who brought you out of Egypt, the land of slavery," as the *first*.

This "prologue" is the precise "gospel" counterpart (and foundation) to the "law" prohibiting "any other gods before me." "Yes" to the true Lord God; "no" to all rivals. "I am the Lord your God, and nobody else gets to have my place."

Jesus warned that we cannot serve two masters. We cannot worship God and mammon, for example (Matt. 6:24). He refuted Satan's temptation by citing Deuteronomy 6:13: "Worship the LORD your God, and serve only him" (Matt. 4:10). The first commandment guides us to say to the Lord,

> You are my Lord and God. I want nobody but you on the throne of my life. You alone, you uniquely, will have this exclusive place in my life.

This is not merely a commandment to *flee from* other gods; it is an invitation to *run to* the God of the universe, the Creator and Redeemer. "I will be your God," promises the Lord, "and you will be my people" (e.g., Lev. 26:12; Jer. 7:23; 2 Cor. 6:16).

What is a "god"?

What is the "god-place" in my life? How would I recognize a god in my life if there were one? The clues come in the statements following the second commandment (and which refer back to both the first and second commandments): "You shall not bow down to them or worship them" (Exod. 20:5; Deut. 5:9). Our gods are the things–or persons, ideas, or powers–before which we *bow down* with our most sincere and profound respect. For what do we *sacrifice* time, money, and effort? What is at the *center* of our lives, giving us *meaning, purpose*, and *direction*? What truly *motivates, awes*, and *inspires* us? What preoccupies us and focuses our attention? What defines our values and our philosophy of life? Where do we look for *salvation, healing*, and *freedom*? What is it that we leap to defend if it is attacked, belittled, or "profaned"? These questions help us identify the gods in our lives.

> It is not the pantheon of primitive gods and goddesses who are the greatest rivals to the Creator/Redeemer at this moment in history but, rather, god-substitutes like Money or the Nation or Race or Gender.[1]

Luther warned against letting mammon (money and possessions) or "great learning, wisdom, power, prestige, family, and honor" rival the true God.[2] In his great little sociology of religion, *The New Demons,* Jacques Ellul argues that the major twin poles of today's sacred are the nation-state and technology.[3] It is to the government that we look for care, for solutions, and for education in basic values. It is in technology that we have faith and hope for medical cures, better food production, longer lives, more meaningful relationships, etc. In the past, people relied on God for healing or for rain. Today, we rely on biotechnology and irrigation technologies.

Probably the greatest rival to God in our era is the self. The gospel of self-satisfaction, personal autonomy, and self-determination is wowing and wooing thousands of converts today. Mammon and material possessions *look* a lot like gods today, but these are often *means* to serve the self, rather than being sacred *ends* in themselves.

In this essay, we want to explore and unpack four rich and powerful lessons the first commandment provides to Christian business managers and leaders. We believe that non-Christians will also usually resonate with these lessons because all people bear the imprint of God's image and likeness and because the law of God is written on their hearts and consciences.[4]

1. God Must Be God at All Times, Including in Our Working Lives

Anytime we narrow our view of God or confine him to particular out-of-the-way corners of our lives, we are in effect "having other gods before us." Every area of life comes under his authority. Jesus said, "If you love me, you will keep my commandments" (John 14:15). This does not mean we will ever be able to serve God perfectly. We are fallen people and can only seek to please him through the power of the Holy Spirit. But our desire should be to grow in our understanding of him and what it means to please him in all areas of our lives.

One way we have other gods before us is in how we set our priorities. Well-meaning Christians have often taught that the order of our priorities ought to be 1) God, 2) family, and 3) work. This sounds pious and right and is often the basis by which we might think we are "having no other gods" before the one true God. But what does this mean in practice? That we should spend more time in prayer, worship, and reading the Scripture than we spend with our family or at work? That our "religious" or "devotional" and "spiritual" disciplines and activities should get more hours than anything else? For most people, this is just not possible. This cannot be what the first commandment requires.

Further, this way of setting our life's priorities suggests that family and work are areas where God is not directly present. We took care of God's concerns first and then move on to family and then to work? But God cares deeply about our families, our work, and everything else in our lives. Separating him from these areas is another way of having other gods before him, as this practice results in us not serving a God who is over *all.* What the first commandment teaches us is that the list of priorities is this: 1) God.

God cares about our worship, our church life, our families, and our work. He cares about every aspect of our lives. He is not a separate priority alongside others; he is the priority in every area of life. He is God at all times. All that we do should be under his authority and done in a way that honors him. It is not God *versus* our families or God *versus* our work. Instead, it's God *in* our families and God *in* our work.

But aren't our worship of God and study of the Bible more important than our families and our work? And aren't our families more important than our work from God's perspective? We believe the answer to these questions is a resounding "No!" If God has called a person to be a teacher, a banker, a software developer, or a construction worker, then this is important work. We cannot trivialize it. When we create these hierarchies, we are acting as our own gods, and in this way, we are having other gods before him.

. . . aren't our worship of God and study of the Bible more important than our families and our work? And aren't our families more important than our work from God's perspective? We believe the answer to these questions is a resounding "No!"

We are not saying that it is okay to sacrifice your marriage or family for your work, or that your Bible study and prayer group are not of great and essential importance. What we are saying is that God is God all the time and in every area. We are saying that creating any kind of abstract hierarchy that appears to partition God off from being the leader of all parts of our lives has to be wrong.

How then do we set these priorities? How do we achieve balance among the conflicting demands we face in our lives? The ultimate answer is that we don't. Rather, we seek God's guidance and authority in our lives. We ask him to help us with our day-to-day priorities and need for balance. We believe this works in two parts.

First, every task we do should be done under his authority and with his guidance. Whether this is in the context of our job, in our family, or during worship, each task at that moment is carried out in sacred trust.

Second, we set our schedules under his authority. We acknowledge that all he has given us to do is "under God" and that we ought to seek his help in laying out the schedule of our days. This doesn't mean we should be paralyzed by the fear of getting it wrong. He has entrusted the work for us to do and has given us gifts and abilities to carry it out. But it does mean that we should be open to his interruptions. We have a schedule, but perhaps an event happens that requires us to do something else. We need discernment to ensure this new task is from God and then to do it willingly, even giving up what we may have thought was the priority.

One of the authors of this chapter was recently on a long airplane trip and had a book he was eager to read. While settling into his seat, he heard a question from the person sitting next to him on the airplane. That question resulted in a five-hour conversation across the country with a young agnostic software engineer. It seemed at first to be an interruption, but it was clearly God resetting his priorities. We need to be open to these kinds of "interruptions" and not treat them as problems but as opportunities.

The setting and carrying out of the many tasks in our lives is a clear way in which we "have no other gods before him." All is done according to his priority, and each task is done under his authority. We break down our own hierarchies and acknowledge God's interests in every aspect of our lives. So the first step in "having no other gods before him" is to recognize God's authority over all our lives—not simply the *spiritual* domain. The God who we worship is one who made us in his image, who gave us our work to do, and who calls us to live our whole lives in relationship to him. He is Lord of all, including our work. When we fail to acknowledge this, we are worshipping a different god.

2. Purpose Motivates and Specifies Ethics

The Moral Architecture of the Decalogue

The second lesson from the Decalogue is that it is God (first commandment) who determines what is good (second through tenth commandments). The Decalogue shows us a moral architecture where God, the Alpha and Omega, *motivates* obedience to the laws that follow. We follow his ways out of love and duty to him.

But the Decalogue also shows us a moral architecture in which the very *content* of that ethical guidance flows from his character. Our understanding of what is right and good flows organically from God's character and will. For example, we observe the Sabbath and work six days out of obedience and love for God, but we do this because God himself is the Creator for six days and the Sabbath-rester for one day. The great French Reformed pastor Alphonse Maillot wrote,

> This commandment is *the Commandment,* the commandment par excellence, of which all the others are only the consequences or commentaries... Thus, in truth, there are not ten commandments but *one* plus *nine. One* true, one great, one alone, and *nine* which develop it, explain it, and show its consequences. This is why I would repeat my reticence before a too strong distinction between two tables of the Law... just as in the same way it is erroneous to separate too much the two commandments of the Summary of the Law. It is fundamentally the same: "you shall love..." God is the one who delivers, and Israel is a

> people liberated in *all* of its existence… Fundamentally there is only one table, that of the new life, that of freedom for Israel… It is not only at worship, not only in my prayers, nor only when I read my Bible that I may not have other gods, but it is in *all* of my life. In my work, in my family, in my political actions, in my relations with my neighbor, there is no question that I could have another God, another reference, another criterion than the one who delivered me from Egypt out of all my slaveries.[5]

The nine commandments are merely elaborations of the first. They delineate nine direct implications of having Yahweh as our living God. If God is truly on the throne of our lives, we will make no idols; use his name respectfully; remember his Sabbath day; honor our parents; protect life, marriage, property, and reputation; and avoid covetousness. There are nine implications of having the one true God in his unique place. As Luther put it, "Where the heart is right with God and this commandment is kept, fulfillment of all the others will follow of its own accord."[6]

This pattern or "architecture" of the Decalogue provides us with an important insight for our participation in organizational, institutional, and business ethics. Learning from this model, Christians should work first at calling attention to the broader, deeper purposes of such organizations, perhaps questioning and prodding them toward a richer and better content. If we can prod colleagues and organizations explicitly toward the justice, love, and freedom of God, that's great. But even if our companies do not commit themselves immediately or explicitly to the service of God in their mission statements, our encouraging them to commit to larger, positive, godly purposes can help leverage better ethical performance in the details of daily work. Anytime Christians can encourage others to address the broader questions of the meaning and purpose of life, work, and business, they have contributed something significant.[7]

Lacking an intimate connection to such an ultimate purpose, much of today's business ethics is reduced to little more than case-by-case "damage-control." Various moral crises, dilemmas, quandaries, and problems spin out of control and beg for careful analysis and creative resolution. Unfortunately, at this damage-control level, our responses tend to be narrow, negative, legalistic, and reactive. The best outcome is pretty much "get through this situation with as little damage as possible." That is hardly an inspiring motive to be ethical; and the very definitions of "ethical," "right," and "good," are at sea. What we need is an "ethics of mission control" rather than an ethics of "damage control."

Lacking an intimate connection to such an ultimate purpose, much of today's business ethics is reduced to little more than case-by-case "damage-control."

Mission Control Ethics

What is the foundation of an ethical organization? Contrary to some common thinking, it is not the company code of ethics. Nor is the key step to hire an ethics officer, or to schedule some employee ethics training. The foundational step is not to create a list of common ethical infractions and start doing some case studies on them. None of the preceding steps will have much power to leverage or guide behavior unless they are intimately linked to a compelling overall organizational mission and vision. First get the mission and vision straight. That's where healthy organizational ethics begins. All moral guidelines with any power to actually lead us point back to, and are dependent on, their connection to a compelling purpose and mission. If we don't buy the mission, we won't buy the principles and rules.

The architecture of the Ten Commandments clearly displays this "mission control" pattern. If God's position is solid and unrivaled, then his agenda of justice, love, and freedom will follow, and we will be formed by the other nine specific area principles.

It is encouraging that some of the best and most popular business books have promoted this sort of mission-control ethics. James Collins and Jerry Porras's best-selling study of great businesses, *Built to Last* (1995), argued that the best long-term companies first "preserve the core" and then "stimulate progress."[8] The order is crucial, they say. The core mission and fundamental values must be the first priority. Collins and Porras define core purpose (what we're calling "mission") as "the set of fundamental reasons for a company's existence beyond just making money. Purpose is broad, fundamental, and enduring; a good purpose should serve to guide and inspire the organization for years, perhaps a century or more. A visionary company continually pursues but never fully achieves or completes its purpose—like chasing the earth's horizon" (77). Collins and Porras argue that mission-driven, visionary companies have experienced greater business success, over longer periods of time than companies that were not mission and vision focused. Max DePree's books, such as *Leadership Is an Art,* make the same point in other language: the leader's chief responsibility is to tell the story that establishes the identity, mission, and values of the company.[9]

Once the core purpose is clarified, the question becomes, "What kind of value-embedded corporate culture and what kind of principle-guided practices are needed for the business to achieve its mission?" What guidelines will get us from here to there with excellence? Business writer Douglas Sherwin explained how ethical values relate to mission and purpose in a classic essay several years ago: "The values that govern the conduct of business must be conditioned by 'the why' of the business institution. They must flow from the purpose of business, carry out that purpose, and be constrained by it."[10] Ethics is essential to fulfill the "why" of business. If the ethical guidelines are not integral to the company's purpose and mission, they will fail. When the purpose is clear, the guidelines are compelling, and the specific dilemmas and problems can best be resolved or managed—from mission to guidelines to problem-solving.

This moral architecture is demonstrated by the Decalogue and biblical ethics. But it is confirmed by common sense and broad human experience, by common grace and natural law. It is the stamp of the Creator's image on all people. It is the "law written on the heart and conscience." Think about an athletic team: only when a team is truly gripped by an intense, shared vision of winning a championship will they sacrifice and suffer through extra workouts. Only then will the players subordinate their individual egos to team interests. Only then will the players study the playbook with total seriousness. Only then will they follow the exercise and nutritional guidelines for exceptional fitness. Only a compelling mission changes team behavior.

Think of how a person's bad habits and long-entrenched behavior sometimes change radically. This doesn't happen very often but, when it does, it is often because that person fell in love and wants so badly to please or win another person that they will change their ways. And think of how in an era of epidemic childhood obesity we see an impressive band of super-fit kid athletes (gymnasts, skaters, basketball players). What makes these kids behave so differently from their peers? A major factor is their vision of getting a gold medal at the Olympics or playing in the NBA. Mission and vision motivate and leverage behavioral change like nothing else.

Negative feedback can have some impact on human performance, of course. Threats of punishment, insults, and shaming can motivate some behavioral improvement in both sports and business. Such negativity, though, makes for a generally weak foundation for ethics (most sexual harassment employee training is of this negative type). Positive, shared vision is much more powerful over time (in raising children, coaching athletes, building nations, or leading organizations).

Toyota watcher and management expert Jeffrey K. Liker describes the first principle of the "Toyota Way": "Base your management decisions on a long-term philosophy . . . Have a philosophical sense of purpose that supersedes any short-term decision-making. Work, grow, and align the whole organization toward a common purpose that is bigger than making money." Liker goes on: "Throughout my visits to Toyota in Japan and the United States, in engineering, purchasing, and manufacturing, one theme stands out. Every person I have talked with has a sense of purpose greater than earning a paycheck. They feel a great sense of mission for the company and can distinguish right from wrong with regard to that mission. . . Toyota's strong sense of mission and commitment to its customers, employees, and society *is the foundation of all the other principles* and the missing ingredient in most companies trying to emulate Toyota."[11] Costco is another great company that gets the priority and importance of mission. Here is how they articulate it in the introduction to their Code of Ethics. *"Our Mission: To continually provide our members with quality goods and services at the lowest possible prices. In order to achieve our mission, we will conduct our business with the following Code of Ethics in mind."*

Mission-control ethics also happens to be the standard way ethics has been understood, taught, and practiced for millennia. Aristotle began his *Nichomachean Ethics* with "The good is that at which everything aims." Ethical/moral goodness is about "ends," and means to those ends. An Aristotelian approach asks, "What makes for a *good* knife?" Well "what is the purpose of a knife?" Answer, "to cut things." Therefore, the virtues of a good knife are things like sharpness, safety, durability, etc. If the purpose of a knife was to be displayed in a museum, things like shininess and color might be among its core virtues; if the purpose is to cut, then sharpness tops the list. Identify the purpose first, then detail the characteristics necessary for excellence in carrying out or achieving that purpose.

So mission and purpose don't just motivate ethical behavior, they specify the *content* itself of an effective ethics. By analyzing what it will take to achieve the mission and fulfill the vision, we can figure out the appropriate values and guidelines. The mission of "cutting things" logically leads us to conclude that the first virtue must be "sharpness." After a business gets its mission and vision straight, it then (and only then) figures out the core values it must embed in its culture and the basic principles that must guide its practices in order to achieve success and excellence. This is, by the way, a common mistake made by many businesses and other organizations, i.e., separating and treating as independent the mission and vision on the one hand, and their core values and ethical guidelines on the other. This, of course, is an alert that the character of that purpose and mission is of decisive importance. If "moving money from your pocket to mine" or "building myself the biggest pile of money in the shortest amount of time" is our business purpose, watch out for the behavioral practices and cultural values that follow from that choice!

We should not be surprised if philosophers, management experts, or any other careful observers of life figure out that purpose and mission drive ethics, or that the End drives the Means. This is a witness to common grace and the imprint of God's image on people. But what is vaguely and intermittently seen in these common ways is explicitly and clearly seen in biblical revelation, and in the structure of the Decalogue and Commandment One in particular. When God is on his throne in our life, things happen. William Barclay commented on the first commandment:

> People necessarily wish to be like the gods in whom they believe, and, therefore, the kind of gods they believe in will make all the difference to the kind of

> life which they live. . . It is of the first necessity to get the idea of God right, for a man will quite inevitably become like the god he worships. . . It is from here that ethics takes its start. A man's god dictates a man's conduct, consciously or unconsciously.[12]

3. Seeing Creation and Redemption as Two Basic Aspects of Godly Purpose and Mission

Let's take the analysis one step deeper by considering who this God is on the throne of our lives. There are many ways of describing God's character, being, and action. He is the Almighty One, the Prince of Peace, the Everlasting Father, and so much more. But if we are to focus on the two most basic descriptions, it would have to be Creator and Redeemer. In the Decalogue, we are explicitly told that he is the Lord "who brought you out of Egypt, the land of slavery (Redeemer), and he is the one who created the world in six days (Creator). The focus on these two aspects of God is reinforced by the themes of the two great songs of eternity praising God as Creator (Revelation 4) and Redeemer (Revelation 5).

The God whom we serve is the Creator of good and beautiful things—and he is the Redeemer of lost and broken things and people. He is the Innovator, Designer, and Builder par excellence. It is in his character; he *is* the Creator. And he is the compassionate Healer, Liberator, and Savior par excellence. It is in his character; he *is* love; he *is* the Redeemer. And every man, woman, and child today and throughout human history has been made in the image and likeness of this Creator and Redeemer. As broken and sinful and wounded as we are, we have some of that creator and redeemer "DNA" in our character as well. The first commandment challenges us to be sure that it is precisely the Creator and Redeemer who is on the throne, inspiring and guiding our values and behavior in the workplace and everywhere.

If a company has a clear purpose but it is a bad or negative one, be prepared for negative ethical consequences. For example, if the mission is really all about maximizing short-term financial payoffs (perhaps especially for a handful of executives), the characteristics that are generated may include ruthlessness, greed, selfishness, cunning, and willingness to step on others. The fall of Arthur Andersen (described in detail in *Final Accounting: Ambition, Greed, and the Fall of Arthur Andersen* by Barbara Ley Toffler) offers a clear case study of how a mission turned bad rapidly led to behavior turned bad and unethical.[13]

> Our mission cannot simply be to "relieve customers of their money." There must be some basic product or service we are delivering in light of which people will part with their money. It is that essential product or service, that change we leave behind in our customer's life, that is our core mission. So, what is it? What does the company want to accomplish? What is the target out there? What is its business in the most basic sense? Only beggars and thieves can have "relieve you of your money" as a standalone mission. A successful, sustainable business depends fundamentally on delivering some product or service well enough to keep customer cash flow coming in. What, in a brief phrase or sentence, is that core product or service? What is the change your business makes in the lives of its customers that warrants their paying you?

Not just customers but employees are affected by our mission. What kind of business mission and purpose will motivate people to want to get out of bed in the morning and bring their best self to work? We believe that an inspiring mission and purpose taps into one (or both) of the two basic theological themes: creation and redemption. All human beings are made in the image and likeness of the Creator and Redeemer, whether they know it or acknowledge it or not.

Creation

When a company challenges its people to innovate, create, and build in some way, it connects with something profoundly human, something God planted in human nature that persists no matter how wounded by sin and ignorance. People are rarely inspired by jobs that have no space for creativity, that ask just for repetition, compliance, and maintenance. There are some classic psychological and anthropological studies of this human characteristic (Latin, *homo faber*, "man the maker"). But it is also common sense and personal experience: think about how good it feels to take on a challenge and have the freedom and responsibility to carry it out. Think of how good it feels to finish the project and be able to look back on it. Getting a book published, finishing a deck building project, running a marathon, completing an acquisition project at work, etc.: human beings are builders by nature.[14]

Great companies tap into this creative "build something good" characteristic in their workforce. Toyota is a model: "Central to the Toyota Way is innovation . . . from the small workplace changes made by plant workers on the shop floor to fundamental breakthroughs in production technology and vehicle engineering."[15] Toyota's development of both the Lexus and the Prius are expressions of creativity and innovation unleashed by a mission-driven organization. So here is the first way we motivate our people to want to get out of bed in the morning and bring their best self to work: we challenge and empower them to express their God-given creativity for something good, useful, or beautiful. Quench, ignore, or repress that side of human personality and we'll watch their lackluster, half-hearted, perhaps even negative performance on the job.

Redemption

This refers in general to setting people free, healing their hurts, fixing their brokenness. The whole creation groans, waiting for this ultimate redemption. This is who God is, the Redeemer who is love and, in effect, can't help but reach out in love to the lost, hurting, broken, and rebellious. We know that every man, woman, and child has been created in the image and likeness of that Redeemer God. No matter how fallen, wounded, and selfish we have become, there remains something in us—most of us anyway—that responds positively to the opportunity to help somebody, fix some problem, or comfort and heal someone hurting. People are inspired by organizational missions and visions that help those in need, heal the sick, liberate those in various kinds of bondage, and overcome hunger, ignorance, or oppression in some form.

Again, there are academic studies of this "herd instinct" and altruism, but the evidence of common sense and observation is powerful enough by itself.[16] Think about how people respond to disasters and human cries for help—there is something in us (most of us, most of the time) that makes us want to help others. When a tsunami, earthquake, hurricane, or terrorist assaults our neighbors, most of us join together to help. When a child falls down or an older person struggles to carry something, most of us step up quickly to help It actually makes us feel good about ourselves to be able to help others. We de-humanize ourselves when we could help someone in need and we selfishly turn away. A viable, inspiring mission and purpose either helps people "fulfill their dreams" or it helps people "overcome their nightmares." Tapping into one or both of these themes is really about aligning the organizational mission with the best aspects of human nature and, more profoundly, with the character of God on the throne.

Create and Redeem:
Some Corporate Mission Examples

The mission of Walt Disney has been a good example of the inspiring potential of the "create something beautiful" theme: *To bring happiness to millions.* While some recent events may give us pause, the broader Disney story has been one of mission-driven, ethical business success. Who wouldn't be inspired to work for a company whose mission is "to bring happiness to millions"?

As might be expected, the great pharmaceutical companies have (in the past at least) tapped primarily into the "help somebody" theme. Johnson & Johnson's mission has been "to *alleviate pain and disease."*

Merck described its mission as *"the business of preserving and improving human life."* As long as, and to the extent that these phrases really focus the mission and purpose of these companies (assuming, of course, a reasonable financial success), employees find these companies inspiring places to be associated with.

Sony's older mission statement was an inspiring statement of creativity with a secondary "help somebody" theme: *To experience the sheer joy that comes from the advancement, application, and innovation of technology that benefits the general public.*

Hewlett-Packard's "H-P Way" also picked up both the creativity/innovation and helpfulness themes. Some of its key elements: *To make technical contributions to fields in which we participate . . . To make a contribution to the community. . . To provide affordable quality for customers. . . To provide respect and opportunity for H-P people, including opportunity to share in H-P success.*

Aligning Misaligned Missions

How do we work all of these out in a setting where we don't have influence over the company's mission? In other words, what does this look like when the mission of our company doesn't appear to line up with God's mission for work, if it is not about creating good and beautiful things for people or fixing broken things and healing hurting people? If we are to "have no other gods before us," we must align our personal mission with God's mission, and this may create some dissonance. Here are three suggestions of how one might respond:

First, we can try to see the work God has given us in a missional light that may not be otherwise evident. The old story of two men working in the middle-ages makes this point. The two men were doing the same job, hauling rocks. One said, "I hate my job. It is hot, dirty work and seems so meaningless." The other said, "I love my job. I am building a cathedral." Barry Rowan, CFO of Vonage, says we need to bring meaning to our work rather than find meaning in our work.

Second, we have enough scope for leadership that we can help some in the company see a connection between their tasks and the broader vision. Bill Pollard, former CEO of ServiceMaster, used to do this for the people who did the dirty work of cleaning toilets and bathrooms in the hospitals where they worked. He had the medical people meet with his cleaning people to build awareness of the link between their task and the larger mission. Cleaning the toilets and bathrooms was an important task on the team that was helping patients get well.

Finally, in our imperfect world, if we can't nudge the company mission in the direction of God's bigger purposes, we may need to do something else in order to "have no other gods before us." Making this difficult call is best not done individually but in a community of believers. We can be blinded by the money from the job, our own egos, or even a misplaced sense of self-righteousness that clouds our own vision. Our families may have needs that make leaving a job especially difficult. Leave or stay, Jesus said that we should be salt and light wherever we are, and working this out in the workplace is one of the most important ways this happens.

4. Treating God and Those Bearing His Image with Uniqueness, Value, and Exclusivity

We saw in the opening paragraphs of this essay that God wants to be our only God. His first command is that there be no rivals allowed into his rightful place: "You shall have no other gods before me." We can call this the principle of "exclusivity" or "the unique place." The Decalogue teaches us that this is the first way we love God, that God has a right to be accorded this exclusive place. He is unique, not replaceable or dispensable. He is valuable, not to be discarded or ignored.

This first command habituates us to a basic pattern of how to treat people made in the image and likeness of God. As we learn to love God, we learn at the same time how to love a neighbor made in God's image and likeness. Our business corollary to the first commandment can be stated as follows: *The first way to love and care for the other is by granting them a special, unique place in our existence and not letting any rivals emerge to threaten or take that place.*

The first movement of love is to make sure people have—and know that they have—a unique and irreplaceable place before you. If they think they are replaceable, all is lost. Children need to feel and know that, no matter how many other people are in the family, they have a unique place in their parents' lives. In a flash, something occurred to one of the authors as he was giving a lecture on the Decalogue to a group of university students about 30 years ago: "This is exactly the first thing that my wife wants from me: to have her place in my life unthreatened by any rivals." (Of course, he knew this about marriage before that night: the new insight was that the first movement of love and justice was the *same* for God, for a spouse, for anyone).

In the case of marriage, you may have other good friends, people you love. But no one should be offered the special place of lifelong soul-mate, lover, and unconditionally intimate life partner that you dedicated and committed to your spouse. While there are many ways of threatening a good marriage, the most threatening of all is to allow a rival to enter the picture, to begin to come between you and your spouse. The point is easily seen in the marriage illustration, but it applies equally to parenting: each of your children must know that they occupy a unique, irreplaceable position in your heart and mind. If they come to doubt that, the relationship is in trouble.

The principle applies in business as well: each of our employees (and customers and colleagues) need to feel valued and unique by their employers and colleagues if they are to flourish. Are they overlooked, dispensable, replaceable, or "just a number"? How will they perform if that's the case? People can usually sense whether we notice them and value their individual existence. The fact is that every person *is* unique in their DNA, in their upbringing, experience, and perspective. Everyone has value somehow, somewhere (even in the case where they do not fit into our organization and must be replaced). Because people are unique, they *deserve*—have a right—to be treated as unique individuals.

David Packard, legendary founder of Hewlett-Packard, wrote, "Our strong belief [is] that individuals be treated with consideration and respect ... Every person in our company is important and every job is important."[17] Stanford business school professors Charles O'Reilly and Jeffrey Pfeffer concluded their major study of personnel and management practices of successful companies by arguing that "These places are also better at attracting and retaining people as a byproduct of how they operate. That is because great people want to work at places where they can actually use their talents, where they are treated with dignity, trust, and respect."[18]

It is not surprising that common sense and experience would lead many observers—philosophers as well as managers—to see the importance of treating people as unique and valuable. Immanuel Kant stated his "categorical imperative" as "act in such a way that you treat humanity, whether in your person or in the person of another, always at the same time as an end and never simply as a means."[19] Don't *use* people as means; value them as "ends."

We don't propose this principle simply based on common sense or expediency, however. We argue that the Decalogue clearly teaches that the first way we must treat God right is by granting him a place that no one else can have and valuing him as he deserves. Because people are made in his image and likeness, they too wish to be so treated. It is important to let this implication of the first commandment permeate us and reform our relationships. We need to pray, "Lord, help me to truly see those around me as you see them: unique, valuable, made in your image. Help me to carve out a special place for each of them in my heart and my affections, my consciousness, and my actions. Help me to value them and protect their place in my life. Help them to know where they stand with me."

This is, more often than we might think, really a matter of justice as well as loving care for others. Our female colleagues, for example, have a right before God to be granted dignity and value equal to that given to men. This is justice, not grace! Our spouse and our children deserve to be treated as unique, valuable individuals; we are not doing them a "favor" when we do so. This is guarding their freedom to be who they are—who God wants them to be. Our workplaces can be transformed by those who live out this principle: "Treat all people as unique, valuable individuals. *Never treat anyone as though they are dispensable, without value, or "just a number."*

Conclusion

It is a powerful experience to relate to the God of the universe and to have no other gods before us. This is not just for us in church or for us in our personal lives. We are whole people, and this first commandment should be at the core of everything. It starts with getting a right and full understanding of who God is. While we can never understand him fully, we at least know that he is God over everything, including our work and business lives. To have no other gods before us means that there is no corner of our lives where we can retreat and not be involved in living this out.

Understanding God moves us to carry out his mission in the world. Serving him *is* our mission. Our work is part of his mission and doing our work missionally is part of what it means to live under his sovereignty. It leads us to an ethic that is much bigger than not doing wrong; it is about doing right and advancing the mission. God's mission in the world involves both creative work and, on this side of the Fall, redemptive work. In all of the work he has given us, we need to "work at it with all your heart as working for the Lord and not for men (Col 3:23). As we pursue and promote godly creative work and godly redemptive work, we are living out what it means to have no other gods before us but Yahweh.

Finally, because every person is made in the image of God, living out our acknowledgment of "no other gods" causes us to treat image bearers of him in a unique and singular way, parallel to the way we treat God by protecting and valuing his unique place in our lives. James and John both remind us that we cannot say we love God and mistreat our brothers and sisters. We demonstrate our love for him in the way we treat each other.

Do the commandments and, in particular, the first commandment, have anything for the marketplace Christian who is "not under law but under grace" in the 21st century? We can't miss it!

Notes

*This article was originally published in the Fall 2016 "No Other Gods" issue of the Center for Christianity in Business's *Christian Business Review.*

[1] Actually, it is not nation, race, or gender per se that threaten God's place but rather *nationalism* (and *Americanism* is no better than *Serbianism* or any other), *racism* (in all forms, covert and overt), and *sexism* (including *genderism* in either of its two potential versions).

[2] Martin Luther, *The Large Catechism,* trans. Robert H. Fischer (1529; Philadelphia: Fortress, 1959), 9-10.

[3] Jacques Ellul, *The New Demons* (New York: Seabury, 1975).

[4] On the ethics of the Ten Commandments see David W. Gill, *Doing Right: Principle-Guided Practices* (Downers Grove IL: InterVarsity Press, 2004); "Ten Principles of Highly Ethical People," *Radix Magazine* (2002) 29.02: 4-7, 27-30; and "A Fourth Use of the Law? The Decalogue in the Workplace," *Journal of Religion and Business Ethics* (2011), vol. 2, issue 2, art 4.

[5] Alphonse Maillot, *Le Decalogue* (Geneva: Labor et Fides, 1985), 22-23. (David W. Gill translation)

[6] Martin Luther, *Large Catechism,* 15.

[7] A general market business ethics book that articulates and illustrates this kind of mission-driven approach is David W. Gill's, *It's About Excellence: Building Ethically Healthy Organizations* (Eugene OR: Wipf & Stock, 2008/2011).

[8] James C. Collins and Jerry I. Porras, *Built to Last* (New York: HarperCollins, 1994).

[9] Max DePree *Leadership Is an Art* (New York: Doubleday, 1989).

[10] Douglas Sherwin, "The Ethical Roots of the Business System," *Harvard Business Review* (Nov-Dec 1983), 186.

[11] Jeffrey K. Liker, *The Toyota Way* (McGraw-Hill, 2004), 37, 71-72. Emphasis in the original.

[12] William Barclay, *The Ten Commandments for Today* (Grand Rapids, Mich.: Eerdmans, 1973), 17-18.

[13] Barbara Ley Toffler with Jennifer Reingold, *Final Accounting: Ambition, Greed, and the Fall of Arthur Andersen* (New York: Broadway Books, 2003).

[14] Nikos Mourkogiannis describes this as "discovery," one of four basic core purposes grounding great companies, in *Purpose: The Starting Point of Great Companies* (Palgrave Macmillan, 2006), 30-31.

[15] Jeffrey Liker, *The Toyota Way*, 42.

[16] Mourkogiannis also highlights this theme, calling it "altruism," one of his four basic core purposes. He suggests "Excellence" and "Heroism" as the third and fourth core purposes undergirding great companies. There is no single way to describe our topic, but, in our view, excellence and heroism are more about *how we approach* "creating good and useful products and services" and "fixing broken things and helping hurting people" (the "two great themes") than separate thematic purposes. See *Purpose: The Starting Point of Great Companies*, 32-37.

[17] David Packard, *The HP Way* (San Francisco: Harper Business, 1995), 127.

[18] Charles O'Reilly and Jeffrey Pfeffer, *Hidden Value: How Great Companies Achieve Extraordinary Results With Ordinary People* (Harvard, 2000), 3.

[19] Immanuel Kant, *Grounding for the Metaphysic of Morals* (1785).

2

Ethical Leadership: An Invitation to Spiritual Formation and Transformation for the Christian Professional

By Doris Gomez

WHEN LEADERS LOSE THEIR SOULS, so do the organizations they lead. From ancient times to today, literature, history, and folklore have chronicled the folly of leaders who, after gaining positions of power, prestige, and status, toppled into the abyss of failure. Many are the sobering witnesses of great leaders—including Christians—who were discovered in unethical activities, thus losing an essential part of their ability to lead. Leaders of every discipline and stature, from politicians, to law enforcement officials, corporate heads, teachers, and clergy, have been accused—and found guilty—of wrongdoing.

The escalation of high-profile scandals and moral failures in recent times in and beyond the world of commerce (see box *Moral Leadership Failures*) has created a renewed urgency to examine organizations and organizational leadership in an ethical context. The birth of an entire ethics consulting industry points to the recognition of the importance of ethics in organizations and their leaders. Sadly, the increasing commonality of "elite deviance," or wrongdoing by leaders, has crept into the cultural consciousness and is dulling down moral expectations and sensibilities. Sayles and Smith coined the phrase "rogue executive"[1] to identify a growing class of leaders who seek and exercise the power embedded in leadership for the sake of personal gain.

Moral Leadership Failures

Politics offers bad leaders, such as Richard Nixon. It also offers evil leaders, such as Hitler or Stalin. The Bill Clinton-Monica Lewinsky scandal and subsequent impeachment trial of President Bill Clinton certainly provided the impetus for a deeper and more critical reflection of ethical standards among politicians and those holding the highest office in the land. Religious institutions contribute their own share of fallen leaders: Jim and Tammy Faye Bakker and Ted Haggard are just a few of the names that come to mind. On the business side of things, the accounting irregularities at Citigroup and Merrill Lynch along with those of Enron and WorldCom are examples of a much larger epidemic of unethical business practices, decisions, and behaviors.

The Shadow Side of Leadership

The choices and conduct of individuals that result in moral and ethical failure have complex causes and include internal as well as external influences. Palmer contends that individuals "for the most part, do not lack ethical knowledge or convictions. They doubtless took courses on professional ethics and probably received top grades. They gave speeches on ethical issues and more than likely believed their own words. But they had a well-rehearsed habit of holding their own knowledge and beliefs at great remove from the living of their lives."[2]

Regardless of the underlying causes, unethical and immoral behavior almost always trigger wide-ranging effects that include an erosion of confidence and trust in leaders and the institutions they represent. This is because a leader is "a person who has an unusual degree of power to create the conditions under which other people must live and move and have their being, conditions that can be as illuminating as heaven or as shadowy as hell."[3] Think of teachers, parents, and clergy who create the conditions people must respond to. And what about corporate leaders whose daily decisions are driven by inner dynamics but who rarely reflect on those motives? As Kets de Vries pointed out, "The road to understanding the dynamics of organizational life is often dependent on understanding what might be termed the inner theater of its key executives: the patterns of conduct that guide their behavior."[4]

Character: The Inner Theater

Increasingly, there have been calls for leadership theorists to explore the inner person of the leader, urging them to strive for wholeness and integrity from the inside out. For example, the theory of authentic leadership[5] focuses on the character of the leader as the driver of positive interrelationships with followers. It incorporates other positive leadership approaches, including transformational, charismatic, servant, and spiritual leadership. Authentic leaders are deeply aware of how they think and behave and are perceived by others as being aware of their own and others' values/moral perspectives, knowledge, and strengths; aware of the context in which they operate; and who are confident, hopeful, optimistic, resilient, and of high moral character. These leaders are as guided by qualities of the heart as by qualities of the mind.

As Warren Bennis noted, "For executive leaders, character is framed by drive, competence, and integrity. Most senior executives have the drive and competence necessary to lead. But too often, organizations elevate people who lack the moral compass."[6] Since character is the inner form that makes anyone or anything what it is, so it is character, guided by social expectations, that is the definitive trait of superior leaders.[7] It is character that allows leaders to face the challenges, triumphs, failures, and temptation of leadership without succumbing to them and responding with unethical and immoral behavior. Leaders who fail are those deficient in traits related to fortitude, integrity, truthfulness, bravery, selflessness, temperance, and moral reasoning. Clearly, mastery of technical or human relations skills alone is insufficient for true leadership. Good leadership is a composite of sound moral practice coupled with professional skills and knowledge.

Therefore, the question—especially for Christian professionals—must not end at "Who is a good leader?" After all, it is quite possible to be an "effective" leader while not necessarily a "virtuous" one. Rather, it must address "How should we live?" and "How do we know right from wrong?" I am increasingly convinced that the answers to these critical questions can only be found in Christian spiritual formation as a central element in the development, formation, and education of Christian professionals.

Good leadership is a composite of sound moral practice coupled with professional skills and knowledge.

The possibility that human beings can be transformed to such an extent that they become a reflection of Christ is central to the message of the gospel, and, therefore, it must be central to the formation of Christian professionals. Spiritual transformation in the lives of redeemed people is a testimony to the power of the Gospel, and it results in an increasing capacity to discern and do the will of God (Rom. 12:2). Christians believe that God is the author and creator of all good things. So it should not surprise us that He also appears at the heart of leadership.

The Spiritual Formation of Christian Professionals

While ethical codes, training, and policies are now common artifacts of most major organizations, they seem insufficient to consistently alter behaviors. It appears that ethics requires higher-order reasoning skills, objective honesty, accountability to someone or something outside of self, social concerns, ongoing self-evaluation, and the abilities to temper emotions, to control impulses, and to delay gratification.

There is a noticeable trend in the management world toward accepting and integrating a spiritual dimension into organizational theory and practice. Spirituality is becoming part of mainstream organizational theory and practice even in the secular world. A number of top companies are making explicit attempts to integrate a more spiritual approach into their management practices, and many leading business schools have introduced spirituality and ethics into their curricula (see box *Examples of Spirituality Integration*).

Examples of Spirituality Integration

The global management consulting firm, McKinsey & Company, determined that when companies engage in programs that use spirituality techniques, productivity improves and turnover is substantially reduced. Companies are increasingly hiring chaplains to support employees. For example, Tyson's Foods has many part-time chaplains at more than 70 sites. Coca-Cola Bottling has chaplains helping employees at more than 50 of their locations. Pizza Hut hires chaplains to guide employees who are struggling with personal problems, and they believe they have reduced the turnover rate by 50 percent.

Marketplace Chaplains USA serves over 450 companies in 44 states and in more than 850 cities. The more than 2,400 chaplains provide personal care to more than 500,000 employees and family members, including well-known companies such as McDonald's, Taco Bell, and Herr's. According to one survey of more than 600 employees at Regal Marine, a boat-building company, the chaplain's care program was cited as the #1 benefit.

The American Stock Exchange has a Torah study group; Boeing has Christian, Jewish, and Muslim prayer groups; Microsoft has an online prayer service. There is a "Lunch and Learn" Torah class in the banking firm of Sutro and Company in Woodland Hills, California. New York law firm Kaye, Scholer, Fierman, Hays, and Haroller features Talmud studies. Koran classes, as well as other religious classes, are featured at defense giant Northrop Grumman.

Marketplace Ministries, based in Dallas, Texas, serves 268 firms in 35 states. The Fellowship of Companies for Christ International, based in Atlanta, has 1500 member companies around the world. They encourage Christian business leaders to operate their companies and conduct their personal lives in accordance with biblical principles. They provide biblically based tools and resources.

Academia has caught on quickly over the years, and business schools have made a great deal of progress in these areas over the past decade. The number and quality of required and elective business ethics courses have grown, as have the extra-curricular offerings and the recognition by other faculty that ethics is a core business discipline. The University of Virginia, Darden School of Business has developed a simulation program that integrates ethics into business decision-making and is required for first-year MBA students. The Wharton School at the University of Pennsylvania has an exemplary program teaching, emphasizing, and integrating ethics in the curriculum, including an option for students to make ethics a "major," noted on their transcripts.

IESE Business School at the University of Navarra in Spain features a Department of Business Ethics, as well as an integrated approach to incorporating ethics into the program. At Harvard Business School, a 2003 student-led symposium challenged leaders to embrace values and explore the bridges between spirituality and business.

Organizational consultants and popular writers such as John Adair, Peter Senge, Tom Peters, Peter Vaill, Steven Covey, and Charles Handy are increasingly explicit about the spiritual dimension of organizational life. For example, Covey states, "I believe that there are parts to human nature that cannot be reached either by legislation or education, but require the power of God to deal with."[8] One author concludes: "The movement to bring spirit and soul to business is no passing fad; it continues to grow and shows no sign of abating. Clearly, something significant is stirring the corporate world."[9]

Most Christians believe that God's Spirit works through all people by what is termed "Common Grace"—enabling them to do good to others and change for the better. In this way, spirituality includes the operation of the human spirit but goes beyond to involve a relationship between the inner person and God. Although most religious traditions describe and proscribe some process of formation, spiritual formation has been a term mostly utilized by historic forms of Christianity.[10]

At its core, spiritual transformation is the process by which Christ is formed in us … for the glory of God, for the abundance of our own lives, and for the sake and benefit of others (Gal. 4:19; Rom. 8:29, 12:1-2). Consequently, Christian professionals must be aware that we are part of an interconnected whole and are here for the sake and the well-being of others. If we want to change that whole, we must change ourselves. Nouwen observes: "It is not enough for (Christian leaders) of the future to be moral people, well trained, eager to help their fellow humans, and able to respond creatively to the burning issues of their time. All of that is very valuable and important, but it is not the heart of Christian leadership. The central question is, are the leaders of the future truly men and women of God, people with an ardent desire to dwell in God's presence, to listen to God's voice, to look at God's beauty, to touch God's incarnate Word and to taste fully God's infinite goodness?"[11] The goal of Christian spiritual formation is, according to Willard, "an obedience or conformity to Christ."[12]

Change and Spiritual Discipline

The Bible overflows with stories of human change. When we compare the change experiences of the people of Israel as described in the Old Testament with the parables and examples of human change in the New Testament, we find a remarkable consistency and congruence. Ever since the fall, God has continually worked to cause his people to realize their utter dependence on him. He does this by bringing us to the point of human extremity, where we have no place to turn but him. As Paul explains in his letter to the Corinthians:

> We were under great pressure, far beyond our ability to endure, so that we despaired even of life. Indeed, in our hearts we felt the sentence of death. But this happened that we might not rely on ourselves but on God, who raises the dead. (2 Cor.1:8-9)

Human pride often holds back change. It is often only when we accept our own inability to solve the situation that our pride is broken and we look to God for change. Oftentimes, the greatest leverage we can create for ourselves is the pain that comes from inside, knowing that we have failed to live up to our own standards. David was convicted by the visit of the prophet Nathan and wrote: "My guilt has overwhelmed me like a burden too heavy to bear" (Ps. 38:4). Nehemiah cried out: "I confess the sins we Israelites, including myself and my father's house, have committed against you" (Neh.1:6).

While outward obedience to Christ appears to be something that we can do in our own power—a cleaning of the outside of the cup (Matt. 23:25–26)—inner heart change is only possible in and through a relationship with God. Christian leaders and professionals have to be informed deeply by the spiritual disciplines that the Christian faith provides us with. While we cannot transform ourselves into the image of Christ, we can create the conditions in which spiritual transformation takes place. This is where spiritual practices or disciplines come in.

Spiritual disciplines are concrete activities that we engage in to make ourselves available for the work that only God can do. This is what Paul is referring to when he appeals to the Christians in Rome to "present your bodies as a living sacrifice, holy and acceptable to God, which is your spiritual worship" (Rom. 12:1) He is saying that we can be intentional about creating the conditions for transformation by engaging disciplines that help us surrender ourselves to God—not just in theory but in reality. As Foster describes it, "[Spiritual] disciplines are the main way we offer our bodies up to God as a living sacrifice. We are doing what we can do with our bodies, our minds, our hearts. God then takes this simple offering of ourselves and does with it what we cannot do, producing within us deeply ingrained habits of love and peace and joy in the Holy Spirit"[17] (see box ***Spiritual Disciplines***).

Spiritual Disciplines

There is generally agreement that the process of spiritual formation is initiated by God, facilitated by the response in faith by the believer, worked out in both personal and communal contexts, with the ultimate goal of holiness as the believer is formed into the image of Christ.

However, even though the process of formation is always initiated by God, the person being formed needs to consent to the formational process through the commitment to practice the "spiritual disciplines" of Christianity.[13] These historic and biblical disciplines of the spiritual life facilitate spiritual formation and are categorized as follows:[14]

a. Inward disciplines: meditation, prayer, fasting, and study
b. Outward disciplines: simplicity, solitude, submission, and service
c. Corporate disciplines: confession, worship, guidance, and celebration

N.T. Wright in his book, *After You Believe*, states that the aim of the Christian life–the goal we are meant to be aiming for once we have come to faith–is the life of a fully formed, fully flourishing Christian character. Proposing a Christian virtue-based answer to the question "How shall we live?" he points to a virtuous circle containing the following five elements: [15]

a. Scripture
b. Stories
c. Examples
d. Community
e. Practices

A spiritual life and Christian character, according to Nouwen,[16] cannot be formed without discipline, practice, and accountability–anything that helps us slow down and order our times, desires, and thoughts on a regular basis and helps us to create space for God in our soul. These include the discipline of the:

a. Heart (introspection and contemplative prayer)
b. Book (reading of sacred Scripture and spiritual writings)

c. Church (community of faith and relationship with the people of God)

While we cannot transform ourselves into the image of Christ, we can create the conditions in which spiritual transformation takes place. This is where spiritual practices or disciplines come in.

It is God's will and delight that we actively resist being conformed to this world and seek instead to be transformed by the renewing of our minds. The Greek word *nous* (translated *mind* in Rom.12:2) includes but goes far beyond intellectual or cognitive knowing. It denotes the seat of reflective consciousness and encompasses a person's faculties of perception and understanding as well as the patterns of feeling, judging, and determining that shape our actions and responses in the world.

Thus, any approach to transformation that seeks to bring about real change must go beyond merely grasping information at the cognitive level. It needs the full knowledge that impacts our deepest inner orientations and trust structures, false-self patterns, and any obstacles that prevent us from fully surrendering to God. This kind of change involves clear teaching about the nature of the Christian life, concrete practices that help us internalize truth in ways that change how we respond in the world, and community that supports and catalyzes the process.[18]

Conclusion

The temptation to compromise basic Christian values—love, community, truth-telling, confession and reconciliation, silent listening, and waiting on God for discernment—for the sake of expedience, is very great. In a high-performance culture (both secular culture and religious) holding to deep spiritual values in the face of the pressure to perform—whether performance is measured by numbers, new buildings, or the latest innovation—is one of the greatest challenges of spiritual leadership. Palmer reminds us that a "leader is a person who must take special responsibility for what's going on inside him or herself, inside his or her consciousness, lest the act of leadership create more harm than good."[19] So, the best and worst thing we bring to others and our leadership is our own self.

The most important leadership tool ultimately is the leader as a person and his or her makeup, and yet this is what seems to get the least amount of attention. Mostly, we focus on professional skills and knowledge instead. The challenges of leadership are both practical and deeply personal. After all is said and done, after all the leadership theory and tools have been studied, leaders ultimately lead according to who they are.[20] Our inward turn, therefore, is not idle self-absorption but is, in fact, critical to our effectiveness as leaders. Leaders must make a courageous decision to diligently examine their hearts to identify areas of needed change and growth. Good leaders do not just focus on the development of the outer competencies required of them at the expense of their inner life. Good leaders recognize the need for both.

Notes

*This article was originally published in the August 2013 "Focus on Ethics" issue of the Center for Christianity in Business's *Christian Business Review.*

[1] Leonard R. Sayles and Cynthia J. Smith, *The Rise of the Rogue Executive: How Good Companies Go Bad and How to Stop the Destruction* (Upper Saddle River: FT Press, 2005)

[2] Parker J. Palmer, *A Hidden Wholeness: The Journey Toward an Undivided Life* (Hoboken: Jossey-Bass, 2009), 7.

[3] *Ibid.*, 9.

[4] Manfred F.R. Kets de Vries, *Life and Death in the Executive Fast Lane: Essays on Irrational Organizations and Their Leaders* (Hoboken, NJ: Jossey-Bass, 1995), xxi.

[5] Bruce J. Avolio and William L. Gardner, "Authentic leadership development: Getting to the root of positive forms of leadership," *The Leadership Quarterly* 16 (2005), 315-338.

[6] Warren Bennis, "The Leadership Advantage," *Leader to Leader* 12 (1999), accessed January 28, 2013. http://www.internetmasterycenter.com/articles/self-development/leadership-advantage.php.

[7] Os Guinness, *Character Counts* (Grand Rapids: Baker Books, 1999), 12.

[8] Steven Covey, *The 7 Habits of Highly Effective People: Powerful Lessons in Personal Change* (New York: Simon & Shuster, 1989), 319.

[9] Paul Wong, *Spirituality and Meaning at Work,* International Network on Personal Meaning, accessed January 28, 2013. http://www.meaning.ca/archives/presidents_columns/pres_col_sep_2003_meaning-at-work.htm.

[10] Kees Waaijman, *Spirituality: Forms, Foundations, Methods* (Leuven: Peeters, 2002).

[11] Henry Nouwen, *In the Name of Jesus: Reflections on Christian Leadership* (New York: Crossroad Publishing Company, 1992), 42.

[12] Dallas Willard, *Renovation of the Heart: Putting on the Character of Christ* (Colorado Springs: Navigator Press, 2002), 22.

[13] Dallas Willard, *The Divine Conspiracy* (San Francisco: Harper, 1989), 106.

[14] Richard J. Foster, *Celebration of Discipline: The Path to Spiritual Growth* (New York: Harper Collins, 1998).

[15] N.T. Wright, *After You Believe: Why Christian Character Matters* (New York: Harper One, 2010).

[16] Henri Nouwen, Michael J. Christensen, and Rebecca J. Laird, *Spiritual Direction: Wisdom for the Long Walk of Faith* (New York: Harper One, 2006).

[17]Richard Foster, "What we believe about spiritual formation," Transforming Center, accessed January 31, 2013. http://www.transformingcenter.org/in/about/what-we-believe.shtml.

[18] Ibid.

[19] Parker J. Palmer, "Leading from within," in *Insights on Leadership: Service, Stewardship, Spirit, and Servant-leadership*, ed. L. C. Spears (New York: Wiley, 1996), 200.

[20] Doris Gomez, "The Heart of a Leader: Connecting Leading and the Inner Life," *Inner Resources for Leaders*, accessed January 31, 2013.

3

Christ-Centered Businesses: Disciple-Making in the Midst of Profit-Making

By Darren Shearer

It is true that business institutions cannot be considered as "born-again," for that unspeakable joy and privilege is reserved for individual people who possess a spirit, soul, and body. However, insofar as certain charities can be considered "Christian" charities and local church institutions can be considered "Christian" organizations—despite that not every person sitting in its pews has been born-again in the John 3:3 sense—businesses may also be labeled as "Christian" in this regard.

Rather than labeling a business—or, for that matter, any other organization—as "Christian," it may be more theologically and biblically consistent to label such businesses as "Christ-centered." Here is a working definition of a "Christ-centered business":

> ... a value-creating, profit-generating, and law-abiding organization dedicated to making disciples of Jesus Christ through leadership by born-again Christians who are led and empowered by the Holy Spirit.

It is assumed that all business leaders want their companies to survive over the long-term, which is only possible through creating value, generating profit, and abiding by the laws of the land. Given the scope of this article, we will focus on the latter two criteria of what it means to be a Christ-centered business:

1. A Christ-centered business is **dedicated to making disciples of Jesus Christ**.
2. A Christ-centered business is **led by born-again Christians who are, in turn, led and empowered by the Holy Spirit**.

1. Dedicated to Making Disciples of Jesus Christ

The mission of Christ-centered businesses is to spread the awareness of God's glory, Jesus Christ, throughout the market-place and beyond.

What is God's "glory"? The writer of Hebrews said, "The Son is the radiance of God's glory and the exact representation of his being" (Heb. 1:3). There is our answer: Jesus Christ is the glory of God. Thus, we can interpret Habakkuk 2:14 as follows:

> For as the waters fill the sea, the earth [including the business world] will be filled with an awareness of the glory of God [Jesus Christ].

In the verse above, Habakkuk has prophesied the fulfill-ment of the "Great Commission" Jesus entrusted to his disciples in which he charged his followers to "make disciples of all na-tions" (Matt. 28:19). Collectively, individual disciples of Jesus are called to disciple entire groups of people—that is, to reveal Jesus (the glory of God) throughout all spheres of all cultures in all societies.

As this corporate disciple-making happens in a business, the business becomes increasingly Christ-centered. In a Christ-centered business, Jesus is revealed through the leaders of the company and, ultimately, throughout the entire culture of the business. When aligned with this disciple-making mission in word and deed, Christ-centered businesses can be used as tools to help individuals, communities, nations, and industries reveal the glorious image and character of Jesus.

Based primarily upon an exposition of the Creation accounts in Genesis 1-2, Van Duzer has proposed that the purpose of business is two-fold: 1) "to provide the community with goods and services that will enable it to flourish" and 2) "to provide opportunities for meaningful work that will allow employees to express their God-given creativity."[1] However, this definition does not account for the disciple-making mandate of the Great Commission that must be central in how Christians aim to honor God through business. Embracing the Great Commission is a central part of what distinguishes Christ-centered businesses from other businesses that are led by well-intentioned people.

In addition to what has become known as the Cultural Mandate—that is, "Be fruitful and increase in number; fill the earth and subdue it. Rule…" (Gen. 1:28)—the Great Commission Mandate in Matthew 28:18-20 must also be foundational in defining the redemptive purpose of business. Only as the mission of the business becomes aligned with the disciple-making, glory-revealing mission of Jesus Christ can we say that the business is "Christ-centered."

With an emphasis on global evangelism and church multiplication, Rundle and Steffen have offered a definition of what they have termed "Great Commission Companies":

> … a socially responsible, income-producing business managed by kingdom professionals and created for the specific purpose of glorifying God and promoting the growth and multiplication of local churches

> in the least-evangelized and least-developed parts of the world.[2]

If "Great Commission" companies are only those operating in the "least-evangelized and least-developed parts of the world," how is the Great Commission relevant to businesses led by Christians in other parts of the world? If, in a business context, the Great Commission is about revealing Jesus throughout all aspects of business—regardless of geography or demographics—this interpretation of what it means to be a "Great Commission Company" is insufficient. Fundamentally, the Great Commission is a call to reveal Jesus individually and corporately, a mandate incumbent upon all Christ-followers and the companies they lead.

In *Business for the Glory of God,* Grudem's objective is to show how various facets of business—such as ownership, productivity, employment, commercial transactions, etc.—can be used for the purpose of "imitating God."[3] For instance, he writes,

> We can imitate God's attributes each time we buy and sell, if we practice honesty, faithfulness to our commitments, fairness, and freedom of choice.[4]

Although Grudem does not explicitly use the "discipleship" language of the Great Commission in stating his case, "imitating God" is precisely the essence of discipleship. As the disciple follows the teacher, the disciple begins to act like the teacher (Luke 6:40).

The more business professionals become aware of Jesus (i.e., becoming increasingly Christ-centered), the more they will imitate him, revealing His image in and through the companies in which they work. Ken Eldred describes such Christians as "role models of a comprehensive gospel," a gospel that provides well-being for both the economic as well as spiritual lives of people.[5]

Cafferky exhorts the Christian business professional to apply the "grand themes" of the Bible in one's daily business ethics and practices (e.g., "holiness, truth, loving kindness, wisdom, righteousness, justice, and others").[6] These "grand themes" are the character qualities of Jesus that Christ-centered businesses present to their stakeholders through their corporate cultures. As these "grand themes" are modeled consistently over time, disciples of Jesus are made as the glory of God is revealed.

Making disciples in the business world may sound more complicated than it is. As with the apostle Paul, a disciple-maker simply invites prospective followers to "imitate me as I imitate Christ" (1 Cor. 11:1). Both individually and corporately, this is a calling to represent and model the character of Jesus as accurately as possible to the world around us.

Discipling Employees: Case Study of Polydeck Screen Corporation

When an employee at the Polydeck Screen Corporation receives Jesus as Lord and Savior, with consent from the employee, one of the company's corporate chaplains provides him or her with an orientation about the Christian faith, helps the new believer find a local church, and helps him or her to get started with Bible reading.[7] Of course, this is only the beginning of the discipleship process. New believers at Polydeck grow as disciples of Jesus throughout each work day as they observe and model the Christ-like attitudes and behaviors demonstrated by their coworkers within the Christ-centered business culture at Polydeck.

How do Polydeck's leaders promote and reinforce the Christ-like character it desires to see modeled throughout the business? One example is the company's successful "I Caught You Caring" program, in which employees can nominate their coworkers when they observe them displaying acts that are consistent with the company's Christ-centered core values. At the monthly gathering where employees' birthdays and anniversaries are celebrated, those nominated are publicly honored and given a t-shirt that says, "I Caught You Caring."

Polydeck's employees also grow as disciples of Jesus by discovering and using their God-given talents daily in their workplaces.

Because Jesus is our standard for excellence in all things, on a corporate level for Christ-centered businesses, the Great Commission is a call to set the standards of excellence in service and character for entire industries. Beyond discipling individual employees within businesses, this is a step in the Great Commission Mandate to disciple entire *nations*.

Discipling Industries: Case Study of Wanamaker's

Through his legendary store in Philadelphia, John Wanamaker (1838-1922) was one such industry disciple-maker, as he is considered the "Father of Modern Advertising." Among his many innovations, Wanamaker opened the world's first major department store because he wanted to provide a store so complete and welcoming that people would not want to leave. In those days, it was unheard of for a store to be a meeting place and even a place for relaxation and enjoyment.

At a time when salespeople could charge whatever they could get from their customers because prices were not displayed, Wanamaker introduced price tags to the retail economy, which was the first universal pricing system of its kind. He didn't want people to worry about whether they were getting fair prices while they shopped. He wanted his customers to be able to relax and feel welcome in his store.

Wanamaker's Christ-centered business innovation led to a shift in the entire retail economy, in effect, discipling entire industries who followed his company's example. He wanted his business to reflect the character of Jesus. This would have been impossible if his customers didn't feel welcome or if they felt they were being taken advantage of by the company.

Ultimately, his gift of hospitality was used to invite people into a relationship with Jesus. When the famous 19th-century evangelist, D.L. Moody, wanted to come to Philadelphia for one of his evangelistic meetings, Wanamaker hosted the event in his store free-of-charge and donated the services of 300 ushers from among his own paid staff to assist with the event. In the same place where these staff members served customers, they heard the Word of God preached to their community by one of history's greatest Christian evangelists.

For Wanamaker, the extent to which he revealed Jesus through his business was his "bottom line."

Specifically and practically, how can a business make disciples of Jesus by revealing him, the glory of God, through the business? This brings us to a second characteristic of a Christ-centered business.

2. Led by Born-Again Christians Who Are, in Turn, Led and Empowered by the Holy Spirit

We can only say a business is Christ-centered to the extent that its leaders are centered on Christ vis-à-vis the Holy Spirit. If a company is in business to fulfill the mission of God, it follows that the company would be led by God Himself. He leads and empowers business leaders through the presence and voice of the Holy Spirit in the lives of born-again Christians.

Here are four ways in which business leaders can be led and empowered by the Holy Spirit, causing their businesses to become increasingly Christ-centered.

Inviting the Presence and Will of God into the Business

To be considered a "Christ-centered business," the voice of Jesus Christ via the Holy Spirit must be of paramount importance regarding the vision, mission, strategy, and tactics of the business.

After Jesus' disciples had been out fishing all night, he instructed Peter to drop his nets on the opposite side of the boat (see Luke 5:1-11). Despite how counterintuitive this would have seemed to this experienced fisherman, he followed Jesus' instructions and benefited from a massive, net-breaking catch of fish that required assistance from other boats and fishermen.

Enabled by the Holy Spirit, this deep level of listening and obedience to the voice of Jesus will be evident in a Christ-centered company. Expressions of this would include regular and ongoing personal prayer times, Bible study, and worship on the part of the company's Christian leaders. Other expressions would include times when the Christian members of the leadership team gather corporately for prayer, Bible study, and worship. These disciplines will prepare the company's Christian leaders to hear from and obey the Holy Spirit at a moment's notice during the day-to-day operations of the company as they make Spirit-led decisions and represent Jesus to the company's stakeholders.

Seeking Wise Counsel

One of the primary means by which the Holy Spirit leads business leaders is through godly advisors to whom the leader chooses to be accountable. The Bible says, "Where there is no guidance the people fall, but in abundance of counselors there is victory" (Prov. 11:14).

There are many thought leaders in and around our industries who we respect for the advice they share. The problem is that many of them do not know God, nor do they share our desires to lead Christ-centered businesses. A diet of business advice and guidance fed primarily by non-Christian thinkers will condition a person to believe that God is not relevant to his or her business. As Larry Burkett said in *Business by the Book*, "The difficulty isn't the advice they give; it's the advice they don't give, specifically, the lack of spiritual insight."[8]

Leaders of Christ-centered businesses give priority to the voice of counsel from those who share their Christ-centered values and mission.

Leading from Spiritual Gifts (Charismata), Not from the Ability of the Flesh

A "spiritual gift" (*charismata*) is a special ability given by the Holy Spirit through a born-again Christian to the people of God for the purpose of spreading the awareness of the glory of God throughout the earth.[9] Because spiritual gifts constitute the anatomy of the "body" of Jesus Christ, who is the "head" of the body (see 1 Cor. 12), using spiritual gifts (e.g., administration, service, prophecy, etc.) literally puts Jesus on display in front of the world. As discussed above, making people aware of what Jesus looks like through the lives of born-again Christians is a prerequisite to making disciples. They must first see demonstrated what they are called to imitate.

Christian business professionals have access to the Holy Spirit's supernatural power in business. This power is demonstrated through one's spiritual gifts, which are individual parts of the body of Jesus Christ. Jesus said, "Apart from Me, you can do nothing" (John 15:5). By choosing to operate with spiritual gifts in business rather than from the natural abilities of the flesh, the business professional is choosing to be completely dependent upon the power of the Holy Spirit. The Bible tells us, "For those who are according to the flesh set their minds on the things of the flesh, but those who are according to the Spirit, the things of the Spirit" (Rom. 8:5).

Fueling Spiritual Gifts with the Fruit of the Spirit

Natural abilities can be motivated by all sorts of selfish motives. They can help a person to achieve extraordinary worldly and temporary success, gaining massive amounts of money and influence.

Spiritual gifts, on the other hand, can only be fueled by the fruit of the Holy Spirit: "The fruit of the Spirit is love, joy, peace, patience, kindness, goodness, faithfulness, gentleness, self-control" (Gal. 5:22-23). For instance, a Christ-centered business leader may operate with a Spirit-empowered spiritual gift of "administration" (see 1 Cor. 12:28) while another may operate with a pride-fueled natural ability of administration. Paul writes,

> If I have the gift of prophecy, and know all mysteries and all knowledge; and if I have all faith, so as to remove mountains, but do not have love, I am nothing. (1 Cor. 13:2)

Our spiritual gifts are useless for making disciples and changing our industries for the glory of God unless they are motivated by love for the people we are serving. Love and the other fruits of the Spirit provide the passion and proper motivation that fuel our spiritual gifts, enabling us to make an eternal impact in the marketplace.

Unlike spiritual gifts, which are given by the Holy Spirit, spiritual fruit must be cultivated in partnership with the Holy Spirit. This "fruit" is the Christian character that each of us must develop over time. These fruits are the Christian business ethics and values we should all be bringing to the marketplace each day. Without this fruit, our spiritual gifts can accomplish nothing for the glory of God in the marketplace.

Conclusion

Until the "awareness" of the glory of God, Jesus Christ, shines into the marketplace through Christ-centered businesses and business leaders, the world of business will remain in bondage to sin and all of its nasty expressions: corruption, greed, poverty, selfish ambition, pride, godlessness, spiritual emptiness, depression, and much more. This provides a redemptive opportunity for Christ-centered businesses. Jesus instructed us to spread the awareness of God's glory, Jesus himself, by being "salt" and "light" to triumph over the decay and darkness in our fallen world (Matt. 5:13-14).

Indeed, Christ-centered businesses must create value, generate profit, and abide by the laws of the land. Though, two distinguishing features of Christ-centered businesses are that they also are dedicated to making disciples of Jesus Christ and are led by born-again Christians who are, in turn, led and empowered by the Holy Spirit.

While the relationship between disciple-making and profit-making is not a difficult one to understand, we must continue to develop a theology of business without making these critical concepts mutually exclusive.

Notes

*This article was originally published in the Fall 2017 "Redeeming Business" issue of the Center for Christianity in Business's *Christian Business Review.*

[1] Jeff Van Duzer, *Why Business Matters to God: (And What Still Needs to Be Fixed)* (Downers Grove: IVP Academic, 2010), 42.

[2] Steve Rundle and Tom Steffen, *Great Commission Companies: The Emerging Role of Business in Missions* (Downers Grove, Illinois: InterVarsity Press, 2003), 41.

[3] Wayne Grudem, *Business for the Glory of God: The Bible's Teaching on the Moral Goodness of Business* (Wheaton: Crossway Books, 2003), 15.

[4] Ibid., 37.

[5] Ken Eldred, *God Is at Work* (Montrose, CO: Manna Ventures, 2009), 161.

[6] Michael E. Cafferky, *Business Ethics in Biblical Perspective* (Grand Rapids: IVP Academic, 2015).

[7] Steve O. Steff, *The Business Card* (Wor-K-ship Publishing, 2015), 143-44.

[8] Larry Burkett, *Business by the Book* (Nashville: Thomas Nelson, 1998), 89.

[9] Darren Shearer, *The Marketplace Christian: A Practical Guide to Using Your Spiritual Gifts in Business* (Houston: High Bridge Books, 2015), 63.

4

Worship in the Trenches: Cases of Christian Business Ethics

By Buck Jacobs

TRUE WORSHIP IS DEMONSTRATED through obedience. In our lives as Christians, our obedience to our Lord defines our testimony and provides us with opportunities to witness the difference Christ makes in our lives. He is seen in the differences. The primary source of our "rules of engagement" with what defines our obedience is God's inspired and written Word. Each believer has the personal responsibility to read, study, discern truth, and apply it. True obedience to biblical commandments and principles is the challenge of every believer.

Christians live in a world of myriad and momentary choices—choices that confront us continually as we process through life situations and the relationships of the "real world." The choices we make combine to form the true Christian witness of our lives. Our testimony is not "optional." Our testimony is what the external world sees as it observes our lives and weighs what it sees with what it hears from our lips. This is as true in our relationships and activities in the marketplace as in any other role or area of our life.

This paper approaches the topic of business ethics from the perspective that the only basis for ethics is from a Christ-centered worldview. As F. Dostoevsky writes, "Without God anything is permissible, crime is inevitable" (The Brothers Karazamov, Part IV, Book 11, Ch. 4). The cases presented here are all real happenings, offered as examples of individuals who strived to apply biblical principles in their lives. There are no presumptions of dogmatic interpretation, nor are the outcomes intended to be perfect or necessarily correct.

Cases

The Gamble

Tom—a visible and respected Christian leader in his church and community, and the owner of a business that supplied components to the construction industry—had experienced six to seven years of substantial, double-digit business growth. He had taken advantage of liberal financing terms offered by several competing banks to expand his business to the limit of his credit allocations.

When the business climate cooled a bit and the market flattened, Tom's creditors tightened the reporting process and required first quarterly and then monthly financial statements. Tom struggled but was able to stay within his compliance requirements for almost a year as the market continued to slow. Then a particularly rough month produced what would have to be reported as a significant loss. Tom feared that if he reported the loss and fell out of compliance, the bank would call his loan. He realized that under the circumstances, he would not have the means to repay the debt and sustain the business.

An option appeared. Tom had a large order from one of his best customers that was due to be shipped the following month. If he reported the sales in the current month, it would change the result from loss to profit and give him at least another month to work things out. The customer had been loyal and consistent, and Tom had no reason to believe that the order would not be shipped as scheduled.

What should he do? Tom's possible options:

1. Call the customer and ask for permission to ship the order early.
2. Just count it in the current month's shipments and hope for the best.
3. Sit down with the bank, explain the situation, and ask for advice.

Helpful Bible passages: Prov. 22:7; Hab. 2:6–7; Ps. 37:21; Eph. 4:25

The Tainted Property

George, the owner of a substantial agribusiness and an elder in his local church, was offered an unusual opportunity to purchase an adjacent parcel of land that would double his holding and potentially triple his revenue. The price was 25–30 percent below what he would have considered as fair market value. His credit was excellent, and terms would be prime minus one percent. The deal was a "slam-dunk," until…

In filling out the loan paperwork, George came to a question which asked, "Are there any environmental contamination judgments or pending violation circumstances on this property (i.e., George's property, which would be the collateral for the loan)? George hesitated. There wasn't any except for a serious spillage of diesel fuel from one of George's storage tanks two years prior. George had researched and applied all the remediation techniques that the EPA would call for, yet he had not reported the incident to the EPA as the law required.

The loan approval process would require an EPA audit. The location of the spill was a bit removed from the primary operations facilities and was not at one of the main storage sites.

Chances were the spill site would be spared from the test. On the other hand, if it were examined and failed the test, the transaction would surely fall through. The prized property would go to his competitor, and George's lie would be obvious.

What should he do? George's possible options:

1. Answer "no" to the question and return the signed papers. The chances for uncovering the omission were slim to none. Acknowledging that he had not reported the incident could throw a monkey wrench in the deal.
2. Go to the bank and explain the situation. Ask the bank for time to go to the EPA and follow their remediation process.
3. Other.

Helpful Scriptural passages: Rom. 13:1–2; Matt. 5:13,14,16; Matt 7:12; Prov. 22:1

The Favor

Four partners owned a specialty chemicals business that was growing nicely. The majority owner (CEO) had come to know Christ four years earlier. He had since shared his faith experience with his partners and they had also become believers. They all agreed that their business should reflect the Christian way of living and committed to doing so going forward. The partners decided to come together and read the Bible and pray before work on Friday mornings. They soon realized that the Scriptures were very clear in identifying them as stewards of God's property. They were convicted of the need to operate their business in harmony with God's commandments, principles, and values.

One Friday, the group was studying the book of Romans. When they read 13:1, "Let everyone be subject to the governing authorities...," someone interjected, "I wonder how the authorities would like our taking liquor orders for the managers at X Corp?" A sudden silence fell in the room as everyone realized that the answer to that question would be very problematic for the business. X Corp. was their best customer, well respected in the industry, and accounted for fully one-third of their business. The circumstance was that the state in which X Corp. was domiciled had a liquor tax that was fully 15 percent above the state where the partners had their business.

As a favor to their customer, the partners would purchase the liquor in their state on behalf of the managers and supervisors at X Corp. and deliver it on the next weekly sales call to the plant. The liquor was for personal consumption only, and the partners would make no profit on the purchase. The CEO had known the plant manager at X Corp. for several years but had never mentioned his conversion to Christianity and his subsequent committal of operating the business in accordance with biblical principles.

What should the partners do? Their possible options:

1. Don't do anything. The small scale of the transgression doesn't warrant a big fuss.
2. Conveniently "forget" to ask for the liquor order next month and hope it goes away.
3. Tell the plant manager that the wives object to the practice.
4. Ask one of the other suppliers if they would like to take over the liquor supply.

Helpful Bible passages: Matt 10:32–33; Prov. 3:5–7; 1 Peter 2:13; Prov. 28:10

The Choices and the Consequences

The Gamble

Tom included the unshipped order in his current monthly result and reported to the bank. The customer subsequently canceled the order and could not be persuaded to take it under any circumstances. Sales for the following month were worse. Tom was forced to correct his statements for the bank and acknowledge his actions. The bank called his loan. Tom lost his business in a Chapter 7 bankruptcy proceeding. His Christian testimony was compromised.

The Tainted Property

George went to the EPA and confessed what he had done. The woman in charge of the local EPA office was so astonished by his candor that she asked why he had taken that course. George said he was a Christian and the circumstances had convicted him of his sin (Rom. 13:1). He was sorry he had not done the right thing and reported the spill sooner. He outlined the clean-up processes he had used and promised to cooperate fully in any testing required. The EPA audited the spill site as part of the approval process. It passed the test. The loan was approved, and George's business has continued to grow and prosper.

The Favor

The partners made a trip to X Corp. and met with the plant manager, sharing their faith experience with him and explaining their desire to live their lives in harmony with biblical teaching. They each shared how coming to faith had changed their worldview and how excited they were to pursue it to the end. The plant manager listened attentively. When they had finished, the CEO said to the plant manager, "We hope that our decision won't prevent you from continuing to do business with us." The plant manager replied, "Do you really think that you have our business because you save us a few bucks on our booze? You have our business because you give us the best product, at the best cost, with the best service that we can find. If and when that changes, you'll lose our business! Now get the (expletive) out of here!" The partners went away rejoicing!

Two weeks later, the 15-year-old son of the plant manager was thrown backward in a wrestling meet and landed on the back of his neck. He was paralyzed from the waist down. When the partners learned of the injury, they immediately gathered to pray for the boy. The CEO then called the plant manager to tell him they had prayed and that they felt assurance that the boy would recover. Later that day, the plant manager went to the hospital to see his son. "Son, you won't believe this," the father said, "but the president of one of the companies that we do business with at the plant called me today and told me that he and his partners stopped work today to pray for you to get well. He said that they were sure you would recover." The boy did recover and was sent home to rest for two weeks before returning to school.

On his next visit, after the business talk was finished, the plant manager reached behind his desk and handed the CEO an oil painting. "My son did this for you," he said. In the drawing, there were two large hands holding up a globe. Across the top of the painting it read, "He's got the whole world in His hands" and across the bottom was the name of the partners' firm. The CEO took the painting to a graphic artist, who created a new logo that his firm soon adopted. Under the stylized globe are also the words "A Christian Company."

Power Tools for Spiritual Warfare

1. Every believer has a personal responsibility to study, absorb, and apply God's Word as a basis for daily living.
2. Seek Godly counsel through accountable relationships with like-minded believers.
3. Learn from experiences that others have had and shared.
4. Keep a consistent focus on the first three.

Parting Thoughts

Obedience often appears to create risk. The author of Hebrews reminds us,

> But without faith it is impossible to please Him, for he who comes to God must believe that He is, and that He is a rewarder of those who diligently seek Him. (Heb. 11:6 NKJV)

Faith means stepping out onto or into uncertainty. Obedience in faith pleases God.

> Behold, to obey is better than sacrifice, and to heed than the fat of rams. (1 Sam. 15:22b)

Each decision we make has significant faith ramifications. The question is always, "What does God say?" Some powerful tools that God has provided in this regard are:

- Every believer has a personal responsibility to study, absorb, and apply God's Word as a basis for daily living.
- Seek godly counsel through accountable relationships with like-minded believers.
- Learn from experiences that others have had and shared.
- Keep a consistent focus on the first three.

We will close with this question: Do we ever truly lose when we obey God?

5

REDEMPTION

By Michael E. Cafferky

SOME CHRISTIANS IN BUSINESS have too narrow a view of redemption. For them, redemption is only about one thing: salvation from sin, in Christ, by faith. Period. Witnessing to this narrow view of redemption limits them to talking only about a theological framework given to concerns about salvation. This makes it easy to talk about redemption in terms of spiritual salvation from sin[1] or the forgiveness of sin[2]. Redemption is about salvation from sin, but it is more.

The biblical concept of redemption is broad, encompassing many dimensions of human experience. Anytime God takes an action which results in a change from worse to better, from misery to shalom, from hurt to healing, or from welfare that is harmed or put at risk to well-being that is improved or made more certain, the Bible considers this redemption.

To understand this better, we must see how the Bible uses the concept of redemption. Redemption is a central theme of Scripture; some would say that is *the* central theme around which all other themes relate. This theme is universal as it relates to all the major Scripture themes. Redemption is presented in a variety of ways in the Bible, yet the basic idea is the same each time: God reaches out to people and delivers them from something that is threatening their well-being. If for no other reason than this, Christians in business will be interested in exploring how this central message and theme is relevant to their work in the marketplace. They will seek to advocate on behalf of a redemption point of view.

Redemption in the Old Testament is sometimes discussed in terms of paying a ransom to buy back someone who is in bondage or to set someone free[3]. The Exodus experience recorded in the Old Testament is the highest example of how God works to fulfill promises while delivering from oppression. Sometimes redemption is presented in terms of removing us out of a snare (Ps. 91:3) or bringing us to safety (Joel 2:32). At other times, its focus is on preserving life (Gen. 19:16, 19). Other times, redemption is when God brings his people from misery to flourishing, from threat to protection (Ps. 18:18-19). Both Testaments of Scripture refer to renewing the heart[4].

In the New Testament, redemption involves spiritual, moral deliverance, healing or being made whole[5]. The experience of Jesus Christ is the supreme example of God's saving power (1 Cor. 1:30). The term uses the economic-laden metaphor of paying a ransom that results in freedom[6]. Elsewhere, redemption seems to emphasize the reconciliation of conflicting parties[7] and deliverance from the oppression of hostile powers. God acts with redemption by finding and saving the lost (Matt. 18:11; Luke 19:10). Redemption is spoken about or alluded to when the Bible writers refer to the new birth cleansing and giving the gift of eternal life[8]. It involves reconciling us in our relationship with God[9] but extends to our relationship with each other (John 13:34-35).

One way to think about redemption is to see it as a grand, overall plan of restoring all things, all relationships, all social structures, all systems. This includes human organizations, our relationships, and our marketplace institutions. Broader still, the Plan of Redemption encompasses not only sinful human beings and the organizations they create, but also the whole earth (Rom. 8:19-22). Thus, redemption is applicable to the so-called "cultural mandate" to create and manage social structures which advance flourishing life.

More than this, unless faith in salvation by God's grace alone moves a person toward *faithfulness in action* and *transformation of character,* such so-called faith is not truly faith (Jams 2:17, 26). Without transformational renewal that results in the faithfulness of our actions, faith is nothing—it is dead (James 2:14-26). Thus, the Plan of Redemption is also about the process of transformation of character, the restoration of the image of God in humans,[10] which is the driver of renewed human behavior. It is here that the day-to-day activities of business can be seen in their deeper significance.

In all these ways, and more, that the Bible either explicitly or implicitly refers to redemption, God is at work renewing, restoring, remaking, and recreating. He invites us to participate in the process in our sphere. At a deeper level, we see the message of Scripture beginning with God's action of creation by which he came to give abundant life (Gen. 1-2). He comes again to renew and restore, that we might have abundant life (John 6:33; John 10:10). At the consummation of the great plan of redemption, he comes again to give eternal life.

. . . the Plan of Redemption is also about the process of transformation of character, the restoration of the image of God in humans, which is the driver of renewed human behavior. It is here that the day-to-day activities of business can be seen in their deeper significance.

Imitatio Dei: Ministers of Redemption

Redemption is multifaceted. If humans are to find their place as ministers of redemption to emulate God's action, it must be in the wider understanding of the concept. The simple reason:

Humans do not have the power of salvation from sin. The Plan of Redemption involves restoring humans in the image of God. It is in this restoration process that we have opportunities to emulate God's character and thereby bear witness to the work of God.

The theme of imitating God (*Imitatio dei*) runs throughout Scripture.[11] Imitating God involves working in ways, in our sphere of influence, just as God works in his sphere of influence. In our sphere, our work involves improving the ability of people and the earth to flourish. One can argue that imitating God involves being as productive as possible but in ways that are consistent with covenantal living. In other words, imitation is not limited to private spiritual experience alone but can be applied to all dimensions of human experience, all moral actions in a social context. If this is true, it also applies to the world of productive work.

Certainly, we imitate God when we participate as ministers of redemption. Whenever we encourage others to respond to the gospel, we are serving as ministers. But in the marketplaces of the world, there are often difficulties that come with openly sharing religious faith. A person might feel free to be open about personal religious beliefs if that person owns the company. But, lacking this level of authority, it is not always possible to openly verbally witness to the gospel in the marketplaces of the world or the corporations. And, sometimes, it is not appropriate to verbally witness to religious faith regardless of your level of decision-making authority. Serving as a minister of redemption cannot be limited to bearing verbal witness to the theological frames of the gospel.

Are there other opportunities, though less direct, to serve as a minister of redemption when you are constrained by the culture of the marketplace? Absolutely! One might even argue that these other opportunities for serving as a minister of redemption are important precursors to direct conversations about the gospel.

Contrast with the Dominant View of Business

The dominant view of business in the so-called secular marketplace, one could argue, is that humans create happiness through market efficiency and making optimal economic choices from among market basket alternatives we have in a situation of scarcity. Humans save themselves through economics, technology, and political processes. If this is all that the Christian sees in the purpose of business, it seems this comes up short of the message of Scripture regarding the Plan of Redemption. In contrast, the Scripture perspective, while not unmindful of the power of humans to influence happiness and our responsibility to contribute to shalom, views business as organized attempts to work together with God in the restoration of his image.

Seeing this from a slightly different point of view, it is faithfulness in marketplace actions where we find the potential of fusing together business activities with religious faith. Fusion is when two things are united in such a way that they are not two separate things any more but instead have become one. We participate as ministers of reconciliation, in part, when we contribute to flourishing life for those around us while we engage in business activities, when we reconcile those who are at odds with each other (a leadership role), and when we allow God's power to free us from the desire to take revenge in business situations.

Application: Redemption in the Human Sphere

We can see redemption (or attempts at redemption) in many places in organizations.

- An entrepreneur who fails at the first attempt (or more) at starting a company finally succeeds after repeated attempts.

- A top-level leader is forced out of an organization by other powerful people only to learn from this experience and emerge as a more effective leader elsewhere.
- A persistent customer is unrelenting in advocating on behalf of what they believe is the truth and is rewarded by a manager who "gets it."
- Workers oppressed by unscrupulous bosses organize and achieve relief from injustices.
- A worker spends his entire career working in so-called menial tasks and learns at retirement that such tasks, when performed to a level of consistency and quality, were what allowed other workers in the organization to have, in comparison, a relatively easy work life.
- A court takes an action permitting a company to restructure its liabilities. This is society's structured mechanism for giving an organization another opportunity to continue serving the community.

Would we be surprised when considering that these are not mere analogies to redemption but instead are examples of how we participate with Christ as ministers of redemption in our sphere of influence?

Seeing the multifaceted nature of biblical redemption, the reader will think of applications in the aspects of business most familiar. The more obvious applications of redemption have been mentioned by other authors, including, to name just a few, Lee Hardy,[12] R. Paul Stevens,[13] and Kenman Wong and Scott Rae.[14] Leaders have opportunities to correct injustices inside and outside the organization. Business professionals can advocate on behalf of the least advantaged in society.

Whenever a person promotes the principles bound up with redemption (faithfulness to promises, loyalty, deep commitment to covenant relationships and other elements of God's character), when a person advocates on behalf of them in the organization and integrates them into personal habits, such a person is telling about the Redeemer just as surely as when mentioning him by name.

Sometimes it is not always clear to the leader which course of action is the one that leads toward redemption. Redemption can work in two, seemingly opposite, ways in terms of human resource management depending on the situation. In one instance, managers who decide on keeping instead of firing an employee may serve as the catalyst for redemption for not only that person but also the entire organization. Forgiveness is a requirement of those who are forgiven. Tasked with deciding whether to fire a worker, the wise manager will look deeper than superficial causes. There are sometimes deeper, organizational reasons why workers act out or are unfaithful to their commitments. Addressing the root causes instead of merely assigning personal blame demonstrates that the organization cares about its people and the extent to which people try to tell the organization that it needs to change. In a different situation, a person fired from one organization is given the choice whether to align with the goals and values of the company. Such a person may find a better fit in a different organization. Redemption, in this case, may have been achieved for both the employee who was let go and also for the organization who let the employee go.

The accountant who keeps careful records which are used later to successfully defend the organization against accusations and litigation acts redemptively. The same accountant who follows generally accepted accounting principles, prevents hundreds, if not thousands, of people from acting in destructive ways to each other.

It is not only people who need to be redeemed and their characters transformed. Organizations, too, need redemption and transformation. Standard operating procedures sometimes need to be redeemed. Look around an organization. Where do we see the need for repairing and restoring the organization to biblical principles so that it serves society in a way that fosters well-being for all, including the earth? This is one reason there is so much interest in developing effective leaders. Left to itself, an organization tends toward entropy, i.e., chaos, lack of goal attainment, and low productivity. A leader's job, in part, is to care for the needs of the organization and its commitment to its community just as it is to care for the needs of individual workers. A leader assesses the situation of an organization and, as a result, makes changes to the division of work, makes adjustments to decision-making authority, or improves how collective effort is coordinated. These and other organizing leadership actions tend to foster redemption for the organization. When this effort is successful, it also promotes redemption to the experience of individual workers.

Caring for the organization, at times, means putting boundaries for employees who otherwise would act in destructive ways toward others. Placing boundaries to prevent bullying or, as the J. M. Smucker Co. does, forbid open expressions of anger among employees, are examples of managerial constraints designed to foster redemption. Managing the tension between caring for the needs of one employee while caring for the needs of the whole group of workers is not always easy. At times, management must place limits on individual requests for exceptions to policy in order to act redemptively for the organization. At other times managers will be flexible with company policies in order to provide for exceptions in a way that brings redemption to the individual.

Salvation involves substitution.[15] Every manager who takes the place of a subordinate, to actually (not merely metaphorically) walk in their shoes at work, acts in substitutionary ways. Every leader who has the strength to bear the blame (take responsibility) for problems rather than shift blame to others acts for redemption. Every time a manager helps other employees see the importance of sharing the work load and making mutual adjustments to responsibilities promotes redemption and teaches about God.

Letting interpersonal conflict fester is like feeding a cancer that will grow until it destroys the whole team. Thus, when work teams or team members come into interpersonal conflict, redemptive leaders will call a meeting and reset the key players to move toward common goals.

While business organizations should not be expected to repair every relationship, business can do its part by healing economic relationships that involve any of the players in the market: employees, customers, suppliers, and strategic alliance partners. Beyond this, a business that operates on principles of integrity and justice plays a key role in bringing stability to all relationships within its sphere of influence.

Redemption involves becoming transformed from the inside out as faithful business professionals. In some cases, becoming transformed may involve thinking more deeply about our work in terms of God's acts of redemption. If redemption encompasses all human institutions and systems, yea all of creation, our work in the marketplace takes on added significance. For example, the person who works in the marketplace in a distribution system has more to do than move product from point A to point B just in time. Each person in the distribution system has a sacred part to play. In the manufacture, distribution, and marketing promotion of necessary products, such as food and shelter, those involved work not only with the things that came from the hand of the *Creator*. These same things and the people who use them were purchased by the *Redeemer*. Because of this, our work in business has a double significance. The cross of Christ is embossed on everything that we need, that we buy and sell, to sustain life. Every house that is built, for either poor or rich, is made possible by the purchase of Christ on Calvary. Each plate of food served at restaurants, in institutions, and in homes was purchased by the Blood of Christ. Every truckload of food traveling from farm to distributor to retailer drives down the *via dolorosa,* whether or not the driver recognizes it. This journey of food (and other products) through the distribution system binds us together in the marketplace in an interdependence that is deeper than that which was established at Creation. We are also bound together by the Cross of Christ. In other words, we are not just agents of Creation but also ministers of redemption.

The cross of Christ is embossed on everything that we need, that we buy and sell, to sustain life.

Final Thoughts: The Purpose of Business

The Bible portrays the understanding that God wants us to use our assets (possessions) to serve others, which includes serving the poor.[16] God's plan of redemption comprehends everything he has created. As imitators of God, leaders in organizations act redemptively toward all of God's creation, including the human forms of organization designed for mutual benefit. Since redemption is a central theme of Scripture, we conclude that it must have something to say about the deeper purpose of business.

The purpose of business can be integral to the mission of the church, namely, that business is a support for a setting in which the gospel of Christ can be extended around the earth. Simply put, the purpose of business, like any other human endeavor, is to be the means by which we glorify God and serve him in ways that are redemptive for the fallen human condition.

Business must be an integral part of the whole plan of salvation, not merely the profession of faith in God for the forgiveness of sins or mental assent to the truthfulness of Scripture. In business, we are not only preparing people to receive the message about the Savior, which leads to initial saving faith. We are also preparing people for and encouraging them to participate in a lifetime process of transformation. Additionally, in a broader way, the purpose of business seen through the lens of redemption involves preparing others for the plausibility that the character of God is relevant to all dimensions of human well-being, including economic activities.

When we review the content of Jesus' teachings in the four Gospels, we conclude that, like Moses in Exodus, Jesus expanded on the character of God and what it means for people in relationships just as much as what it means for God's relationship with us. Participating in redemption involves something larger and deeper than teaching about doctrine, even if that doctrine is the doctrine of salvation. It also means *showing* the character of God in action, central to which is the desire to redeem.

Notes

*This article was originally published in the Fall 2017 "Redeeming Business" issue of the Center for Christianity in Business's *Christian Business Review*.

[1] Matthew 1:21; John 1:29; Acts 4:12; Romans 5:14-17.

[2] Ephesians 1:7; Colossians 1:14.

[3] Exodus 6:6; Psalm 77:14-15.

[4] Psalm 51:10; Jeremiah 32:39; Ezekiel 11:19-20; Romans 6:4; 1 John 3:2.

[5] Matthew 1:21; Luke 1:69; 19:9; Acts 13:47; Romans 1:16.

[6] 1 Corinthians 6:20; Romans 3:24; Ephesians 1:7.

[7] Acts 15; 2 Corinthians 5:19; Romans 5:10-11; Ephesians 2:16.

[8] See John 3:3-5; 1 Peter 1:23; 1 John 2:29 with reference to new birth; cleansing: 1 Corinthians 6:11; Ephesians 5:26; Titus 3:5; and gift of eternal life: John 3:16; Romans 5:21; Romans 6:23.

[9] Romans 5:10; 2 Corinthians 5:18-20; Colossians 1:22.

[10] 2 Corinthians 5:17; Ephesians 4:24; Colossians 3:10.

[11] See, for example, Leviticus 11:45; 19:2; 20:7; Matthew 5:48; Luke 6:36; John 13:15; Ephesians 4:23-24; 5:1; Philippians 2:2-11.

[12] Lee P. Hardy, *The Fabric of This World: Inquiries into Calling, Career Choice, and the Design of Human Work* (Grand Rapids, MI: Wm. B. Eerdmans Publishing Co., 1990).

[13] R. Paul Stevens, *Doing God's Business: Meaning and Motivation for the Marketplace* (Grand Rapids, MI: Wm. B. Eerdmans Publishing Co., 2006).

[14] Kenman L. Wong and Scott B. Rae, *Business for the Common Good: A Christian Vision for the Marketplace* (Downers Grove, IL.: InterVarsity Press, 2011).

[15] See Mark 10:45; Matthew 26:28; Mark 14:24; Hebrews 9:22; Romans 4:25; Romans 8:32; Galatians 2:20; Ephesians 5:2.

[16] See Deuteronomy 15:8; Psalm 112:5-9; Proverbs 19:17; Isaiah 58:7; Matthew 5:42; Luke 12:33.

6

Transformational Stewardship

By Bill Mearse

UPON HEARING THE WORD "stewardship," many parishioners reach for their wallets, checkbooks, or debit cards (depending on their generation) to financially support church ministries. In the secular arena, people refer to responsible citizenship when giving time and resources to various non-profit causes. The reality is stewardship represents a transformational biblical principle that provides individuals and organizations the impetus for growth well beyond their own potential.

Stewardship involves living for a higher, broader purpose to foster a greater, lasting outcome. A narrow view implies the completion of an obligation to fulfill a specific expectation. The broader perspective creates results that exceed expectations. Ultimately, stewardship involves people giving their lives to God for outcomes greater than their capabilities, larger than their footprints, and lasting longer than their lifetimes.

Stewardship in Context

The traditional American dream reflects stewardship by providing the next generation of our families with better opportunities for success. Parents enable these opportunities by providing a better education, breaking destructive behavioral cycles, or leaving a stronger balance sheet.

My generation was the first on both sides of our family to attend college. Despite no precedents, my parents unequivocally planned for my brother and me to earn a college degree. Their personal sacrifices enabled our college graduation, meaningful business careers, and better opportunities for our families. For the American dream to continue, people need to nurture stewardship within families.

Private and public organizations generate value by using stewardship to facilitate strong financial performance, meaningful employee engagement, and impactful community service. For example, global consultancy Accenture's core values include stewardship defined as: "Fulfilling our obligation of building a better, stronger, and more durable company for future generations, protecting the Accenture brand, meeting our commitments to stakeholders, acting with an owner mentality, developing our people and helping improve communities and the global environment."

. . . stewardship involves people giving their lives to God for outcomes greater than their capabilities, larger than their footprints, and lasting longer than their lifetimes.

As an Accenture employee for almost 34 years, I experienced the influence of stewardship on the mindset of this organization. Accenture's leadership and employees have always discussed the importance of leaving the company in better shape than when they started. While the manifestations of stewardship may differ by individual, this core value has created a unique and bonding culture across Accenture's global operations and generations of employees.

The Bible articulates the true expectations for stewardship in our lives. Stewardship involves faithful tithing as specified in the Old Testament (Mal. 3:10) and purpose-driven, cheerful giving as described in the New Testament (2 Cor. 9:7).

Limiting stewardship to monetary matters, however, narrows its potential for changing lives. Giving all aspects of our life to Jesus Christ empowers the full potential of stewardship by acknowledging all we have comes from and belongs to God.

Since making this decision as a teenager, I have experienced the power of stewardship by seeking His purpose (Col. 3:17), His plans (Jer. 29:11), and His desires (Gal. 2:20) for my life. Despite my personal shortcomings, the opportunities and accomplishments God has provided have exceeded all my own aspirations, and I remain confident the best is yet to come (Phil. 1:6).

Stewardship Mandates

Stewardship seeks opportunities not entitlements—a privilege not a right.

This mindset embraces fulfillment of potential versus satisfaction of the status quo. Craig Biggio exemplifies this stewardship quality. After making the 1991 All-Star team as a catcher, the Houston Astros asked Craig to change positions. Accepting this challenge, Craig became an All-Star as a second baseman six out of seven years beginning in 1992. At the request of the Astros, Craig also played centerfield during 2003–04 to increase the team's chance of winning before finishing his career in 2007, having played his entire career in Houston. Craig demonstrated stewardship by placing team success above his own and leaving a legacy for future generations of Astros as a Hall of Fame inductee.

Stewardship views risk as an investment, not an expense—value versus cost.

This focus emphasizes a long-term perspective rather than short-term fears. For instance, the investment horizon for oil and gas companies can approach 10+ years. While short-term market factors may adversely impact annual capital expenditures, their commitment to the long-term remains steadfast.

The Bible also illustrates this point with a man who entrusted his servants with specific monetary amounts before departing on a trip, giving one ten talents, another five talents, and a third one talent. When he returned, this man met with his servants to review the status of their investments. The servants with ten and five talents both had doubled their original amounts, but the servant with one talent had done nothing for fear of losing it. This servant still lost his talent, as the man gave it to the one who originally had ten (Matt. 25:14-30). For Christians, the long-term returns of stewardship last for eternity.

Stewardship requires an ownership mentality that creates a strong sense of responsibility and accountability.

Human nature often causes people to care less about items they rent versus own. Reliable stewards treat the possessions of others with the same diligence as their own. As an example, consultants who excel at Accenture develop a strong client perspective by learning all aspects of the company and its industry—as if an owner. By identifying key value levers and challenges, these consultants can shape opportunities to optimize their client's business performance. While balancing the interests of both parties, this approach assumes delivering value for the client will also benefit Accenture by creating a trusted, long-term relationship and a stronger economic proposition. In the same way, placing the interests of God ahead of our own results in a stronger commitment and a greater impact than if we pursue only our own desires.

Stewardship realizes influence proves more effective than authority.

Influence involves demonstrated capability and established credibility, resulting in trusting relationships. These relationships provide the basis for influence. Expanding spheres of influence proves more important as careers progress because organizations often expect people to deliver results beyond their level of authority.

During my tenure with Accenture, I served in numerous internal roles—some empowered with "line" authority while others relied on personal influence. In addition, clients rarely empowered me with the authority to meet their full expectations. Effective influence demonstrates a "solve for Accenture (or client) first" mindset above personal interests. Consistently showing this mentality builds trust, enabling influence to grow over time. In fact, most leaders prefer to affect change through influence rather than authority to foster faster and broader acceptance within the organization. Christian stewardship often leverages the influence of the Holy Spirit to present opportunities and resolve circumstances through various "coincidences" in our lives.

Stewardship focuses on motivation more than circumstances.

Successful people seek to fulfill high expectations—pursue a mission versus complete a task. These expectations enable a positive attitude despite periodic challenges. Playing 19 years for the Chicago Cubs, Ernie Banks experienced only six winning seasons and holds the record for the most games played without a postseason appearance. Despite this lack of team success, Ernie earned two National League Most Valuable Player awards, played in 14 All-Star games, and became a Hall of Fame inductee. Ernie also displayed an ever-optimistic attitude exemplified by his infamous line of "let's play two" and received the Presidential Medal of Freedom in 2013. Similarly, Christian missionaries demonstrate stewardship by submitting their lives to sacrificial service, often under difficult and challenging circumstances, receiving the joy of the Lord rather than the accolades of this world.

Measures of Stewardship

You get what you measure. This adage stresses the importance of defining and assessing effective metrics to facilitate desired results. The following measures provide evidence of stewardship:

- *Confidence*—involves how (tone) and what (content) we say.
- *Credibility*—demonstrates alignment between what we do versus what we say.
- *Respect*—reflects the attitude that the ends do not justify the means.
- *Trust*—reflects our motives, reiterating why we do something is more important than what we do.
- *Patience*—shows maturity to wait for right outcomes in a world demanding instant gratification.
- *Commitment*—maintains focus on purpose despite obstacles and challenges.

The life of Joseph illustrates these measures of stewardship. His sense of God's calling through dreams served as Joseph's source of confidence as a young boy. These dreams alienated him from his brothers, who sold Joseph to an Egyptian caravan. Arriving in Egypt, Joseph displayed credibility by refusing the seduction of Potiphar's wife. Despite his loyalty, Potiphar imprisoned Joseph after his wife's false accusations of sexual misconduct.

While in prison, Joseph demonstrated patience by serving the chief jailer and accurately interpreting dreams for Pharaoh's imprisoned baker and cupbearer. Several years later, Pharaoh could not find someone to interpret his dreams until the cupbearer remembered Joseph. Through his professed reliance on God for his divine discernment of dreams, Joseph earned the respect and trust of Pharaoh, who granted him authority over all of Egypt.

When the sons of Jacob came to Egypt seeking grain during the seven years of famine, Joseph recognized the fulfillment of his commitment. While the actions of his brothers resulted from evil, God transformed their actions for good by placing Joseph in a position to save his family.

Implementing the Stewardship Mandates

Defining a strategy or designing a concept can present some challenges; however, the implementation phase often proves more difficult as theory and assumptions collide with reality. In the same way, discussing stewardship is easier than demonstrating stewardship.

Nehemiah illustrated several principles for effectively implementing stewardship while leading the Jewish people to rebuild the walls of Jerusalem:

Establish stewardship as a core value.

This step aligns aspirations and expectations with mindsets and behaviors. The sense of a higher purpose creates a mission with a larger and longer lasting impact. Stewardship facilitates a calling that requires dependency on God for success.

While holding an important position and living hundreds of miles away in Persia, Nehemiah sensed God's calling to rebuild the walls of Jerusalem. Despite the magnitude and risk, Nehemiah answered this calling by seeking and relying on God to secure the sponsorship of the Persian king for safe travel and resources.

Empower stewardship through servant leadership.

Solving for a broader purpose ahead of personal gain unleashes the power of stewardship. Servant leaders facilitate the growth of others by removing obstacles to their success. This process reinforces the value of stewardship among others and shares the fruits of success accordingly.

Nehemiah arrived in Jerusalem with no fanfare and maintained a low profile while assessing the situation. His approach enhanced the preparation for rebuilding the walls while also confirming the nature of his motives. Recognizing his higher sense of calling, the people accepted the challenge presented by Nehemiah.

Encourage stewardship among others.

Sharing common aspirations creates synergy, resulting in joint outcomes that exceed the sum of individual ones. When aspirations involve a unified faith in God, stewardship becomes an evangelistic agent permeating lives to overcome challenges and delivering supernatural results.

Amidst ridicule and threats, the Jews began to rebuild the walls of Jerusalem. Nehemiah continuously encouraged everyone while adapting tactics to offset the opposition. Completing the rebuilding process in 52 days exceeded the expectations and capabilities of the people who heeded God's leadership and leveraged Nehemiah's stewardship.

Conclusion

Stewardship involves living for a higher, broader purpose to foster a greater, lasting outcome. As the ultimate example of stewardship, a king vacated his throne to reside among his subjects to give them a better life. Through this experience, the king disguised his identify and relinquished his privileges. The people did not recognize him and rejected his approach to a better life. Their rejection became hostile, resulting in humiliation, suffering, and eventually a cruel, horrific death.

Stewardship involves living for a higher, broader purpose to foster a greater, lasting outcome.

The people, however, did not realize his death was part of the plan. In fact, his sacrifice and subsequent resurrection empowered forgiveness for their rejection and created hope of an everlasting legacy. The name of this king is Jesus Christ. Accepting His stewardship transforms our lives for the day when every knee will bow before him and every tongue will confess his identity (Phil. 2: 3-11). The reality of His stewardship makes the potential for our stewardship a reality.

Notes

*This article was originally published in the Fall 2015 "Focus on Stewardship" issue of the Center for Christianity in Business's *Christian Business Review.*

7

Animal Spirits vs. The Holy Spirit: Worldviews and Financial Crises

By Ernest P. Liang

IN FINANCIAL MARKETS, volatility (asset price gyrations) is synonymous with risk. Heightened risk perception discourages participation by market investors and precipitates speculative trading, leading to more volatility, rising risk premiums, and depressed asset prices.[1] The decade that began in the year 2000 is often labeled the "lost decade" because the burst of the internet and subprime housing bubbles, along with the after effects of the 9/11 and global credit crises, brought about one of the worst ten-year investment periods ever for stocks.[2] Market volatility was inarguably a contributor to the market's performance malaise, but what were the drivers of runaway, spontaneous volatility that can and have plunged markets and entire economies into a tailspin?

The experience of the last decade has put the spotlight on the fundamental role of the human psyche in the recurrent cycles of financial and economic crises. Human emotions and passions—greed, fear, excitement, and hope—offer unique insights into why markets spiral into euphoria and panic against rational expectations.[3] As one analyst observed during a particularly volatile time in recent market history, "Macro factors and psychology are the most important factors for investors right now."[4] The behavioral perspective on markets also convinced some scholars that future crises will be difficult, if not impossible, to eliminate.[5]

. . . but what were the drivers of runaway, spontaneous volatility that can and have plunged markets and entire economies into a tailspin?

While human psychology contributes to a better understanding of market upheavals, it does not help resolve problems that are beyond human self-control. The nature of man and his relationships are the basic substance of both the behavioral sciences and the Holy Scriptures, and it is the latter that can offer a definitive solution to the intractable ills of the human psyche. Policymakers who don't share a biblical worldview would arrive at drastically different conclusions than those who do. If humans are but evolved animals with higher intelligence, then human passions and the behaviors they manifest are spontaneous expressions of our animal spirit. These expressions need to be constrained, coaxed, and perhaps channeled by laws toward the common good. Accordingly, much emphasis has been placed by secular scholars and policymakers on the role of the state, by engaging tools of legislation, regulation, ethical education, and public awareness campaigns, as key pillars for any meaningful solutions.

If, instead, humans are made in God's image and bear a conscience redeemable by faith, then Christian virtues would play a significant role in sustaining the robustness of modern market systems. As Logue observed, "(Christian) virtues and virtuous behavior make markets more efficient and that sufficient integrity must exist to engender a critical level of trust or markets will completely collapse."[6] This suggests that any solution which ignores the life-transforming power of the Holy Spirit does not address the core issues of human frailty and will necessarily fall short. As theologian Carl Henry observed back in 1955: "The disengagement of economic problems from the spiritual realm, the determination to find economic solutions while the religious problem is ignored or held in suspense, constitutes the prime crisis."[7]

This essay suggests that a comprehensive solution to market turbulence and financial crises is not found in a behavioral theory of the will, but rather one of the heart—one that is transformed and renewed day by day in a Spirit-filled life. Human frailties, the psychological underpinnings of cycles of booms and busts, can be met in the end only by spiritual answers. Biblical revelation, which gives unique insights into the nature and experience of the human soul or psyche, offers the only kind of wisdom that can restore hope and redress deficiencies that lie at the heart of financial and economic crises.

Financial Crises and the Nature of Man

Historic cycles of market manias, panics, and crashes are a hardy perennial in world financial history and share features with much commonality.[8] From the Dutch Tulip mania and the South Sea and Mississippi bubbles in the 17th and early 18th centuries, to the parade of regional and global financial crises since the 1980s, financial panics and the associated economic maelstroms are marked by almost uniform undercurrents of excesses in liquidity, leverage, and risk-taking.[10]

The concept of "excesses" or "manias," however, suggests a loss of touch with rationality, a basic tenet of (neo)classical economics. Economic self-interest in the classic (Adam) Smithian sense is understood to promote fair and orderly (i.e., confident) markets.[9] The rational expectations assumption in economics postulates that asset prices are generally "right" in efficient markets, making excesses and frenzied reactions to changes in economic conditions unsustainable and expeditiously self-correcting events.[11] While affirming rationality as a useful and generally valid description of reality, economists do allow for occasional departures from this assumption when rational individuals succumb to some type of "group think," "mob psychology," or "hysteria."[12]

One widely recognized thread that strings together historical episodes of economic upheaval is traced, not surprisingly, to the very nature of man. Humans are at the same time rational and irrational decision-makers. The rational man is driven by a deliberative assessment of options based on an informed, timely, forward-looking evaluation of relevant costs and benefits. The affective man, who behaves purely in response to innate passions such as optimism, pessimism, anger, greed, and fear, is anything but rational.[13]

Historically, both patterns of behavior play a role in the boom-bust cycles of the financial world. Creative innovations that advance markets, improve trade, reduce risk, and create wealth were inevitably products of the resourceful, evaluative utility maximizer. Yet activities that take advantage of such innovations often spring from spontaneous responses to affective stimuli encompassing emotions and knee-jerk reactions aroused by basic instincts. For example, the growth of complex, often highly leveraged, financial instruments known as derivatives have taken financial trading by storm since the 1970s. Derivatives make markets more efficient because they allow for the efficient transfer of risk between market participants. But often, "derivatives were a simple case of greed and fear. Clients used these instruments to make money (greed) or protect themselves from the risk of loss (fear). Frequently, they confused the two."[14]

In today's modern economies, financial innovations have enabled massive transactions of highly leveraged speculative positions. The frequency of spiking volatility and convulsive reactions in financial markets seem to have multiplied since the turn of the new millennium as increasingly complex instruments and high frequency trading enable sharply amplified returns of investments with increasingly shortened time horizons.[15] As a result, markets have become increasingly seized with "hysteria" as investors react in knee-jerk reflex to opinions, speculations, or rumors, especially when the macroeconomy is at an inflexion point.[16]

Animal Spirits and Economic Crises

John Maynard Keynes, the namesake of Keynesian economics, first referenced the term "animal spirit" when describing the emotive state of human nature in economic decision-making. In his seminal work, *The General Theory,* Keynes suggests that "most of our decisions...can only be taken as the result of animal spirits—a spontaneous urge to action rather than inaction, and not as the outcome of a weighted average of quantitative benefits multiplied by quantitative probabilities."[17] According to Keynes, "animal spirit" is a persistent, predictive cause of economic instability. More recently, Nobel laureates George Akerlof, and Robert Shiller concluded in their book, *Animal Spirits: How Human Psychology Drives the Economy,* that "economic crises are caused by changing thought patterns...by our changing confidence, temptation, envy, resentment, illusion, and ... stories."[18] According to these scholars, by ignoring the role of animal spirits, the rationality assumption blinds us to the most important dynamics underlying economic crises and a path to effective responses.

Within the moral framework, the struggle between emotive and rational behaviors finds a close parallel in Adam Smith's contests between "passions" and "the impartial spectator," and in the Bible, the apostle Paul's incessant tug-of-war between "flesh" and "spirit." Adam Smith, in *The Theory of Moral Sentiments,* identifies the impartial spectator as the human ability to take a dispassionate view of one's own conduct, as the source "of self-denial, of self-government, of that command of the passions."[19] Yet he recognizes that such perspective-taking can be overcome by sufficiently intense passions which "the greatest degree of self-government is not able to stifle."[20]

For the apostle Paul, the "flesh," being the embodiment of the intellectual and moral frailties of fallen humanity, does and desires no good (Gal. 5:19-21). It is dominated by "fleshly passions" (Rom. 7:5) and is unable to obey God's law (Rom 8:3). The "spirit," on the other hand, is the new self, created in righteousness and holiness of the truth (Eph. 4:22-24). Driven by the presence of God in man (Gal. 4:6, Rom. 8:15), the regenerated self is dominated by disciplined living that seeks to please God. These two principles are in deep and irreconcilable conflict, "for the flesh sets its desire against the Spirit, and the Spirit against the flesh; for these are in opposition to one another, so that you may not do the things that you please" (Gal. 5:17).

These moral perspectives suggest that the torrent of "irrational" behaviors and moral indiscretions when reasoned responses and self-denial should be expected reflects the nature of the "flesh" at work. According to secular analysts, animal spirits (i.e., "flesh") are intrinsic to human nature. Individuals are basically incapable of making or unwilling to make proper economic decisions for themselves.[21] Hence, paternalistic government programs and policies must step in to save people from making mistakes. In other words, artificial restraints of the will are needed to steer human behaviors and to rein in raging passions when they flare up. To quote Akerlof & Shiller, "The proper response lies with the state executing interventions so that animal spirits can be harnessed creatively to serve the greater good, [and thus] … (the) government must set the rules of the game."[22]

The main difficulty with this prescription, however, is that "animal spirits" also pervade government institutions and regulators so that they are as susceptible to panics and manias as in the private sector. In addition, policymakers almost always overestimate the impact of a new law or policy intended to constrain human behavior. Evidence abounds that such constraints often generate behavior which was never imagined by its sponsor. As Michael Jensen and William Meckling, two pioneers of modern finance, concluded: "As resourceful and evaluative maximizers, individuals respond creatively to the opportunities the environment presents, and they work to loosen constraints that prevent them from doing what they wish."[23] In other words, rules that merely seek to constrain rather than incentivize modified behavior often fail to yield expected results because of the creativity of the resourceful, rational human being.

The past half century offers many illustrations of how newly imposed constraints by the state fumbled in the face of rational responses from those being impacted. It is well documented that practices such as regulatory arbitrage and loophole mining have been used effectively by impacted market participants to frustrate attempts of governmental intervention.[24] According to Miller, the exploitation of regulatory inconsistencies has indeed been a major impetus for financial innovations.[25] Over time, such innovative responses multiplied the sophistication of financial instruments, greatly enhanced the complexity of trades, and spawned shrewdly adaptive market intermediaries. Inevitably, future crises would expand in scope and intensity with each recurrence and will be met by an ever-stronger regulatory response from the state. Such innovation-regulation response cycles will cease to spiral only when the institution gets so asphyxiated by the regulatory morass that it finally collapses under its own weight.

If humans are creative, rational adaptors to artificial restraints as history seems to suggest, then the wisdom to deflect future financial crises is unlikely to be found in the goodwill or discipline of human institutions. In a post-modern world in which "religious belief" is but a matter of "personal feelings" (i.e., emotions, passions),[26] humanistic "moral" suasion also rings hollow. The "good" of human action, in the absence of ascendant accountability, is but one variable, if at all, in the economic calculus of risk and return.[27] A worldly wisdom devoid of a transcendent God to whom all are accountable in eternity is the ultimate source of confidence loss,[28] the very trigger of panics and manias. But there is a better alternative, one found in the spiritual-moral moorings laid down by a higher, supernatural authority—the Creator, God. As Carl Henry observed, "Separate the economic sphere from the living God and His claims, and humans will drift from one crisis to another under any economic formula."[29]

Godly Wisdom and the Holy Spirit

Godly wisdom pertains to a regenerated spiritual person who leads a principled life that is not captive to fleshly passions. Godly wisdom, according to the Scripture, is especially associated with the Holy Spirit as a gift from God and comes by revelation (1 Cor. 2:4-6, Eph. 1:17, James 1:5). The wisdom that is derived from human knowledge brings only grief and frustration (Eccl. 2:9-11), and the confidence and pride that are bred from such knowledge lead only to destruction (1 Cor. 1:19-20, Ezek. 28:2-9).

In the final analysis, the wisdom that can solve the problems of human weaknesses must be the wisdom that applies divine truths to the human experience. This wisdom, as Proverbs 9:10 declares, is based on the "fear of the Lord," a fear out of reverence that requires a personal knowledge of the Almighty. This divine wisdom keeps the commandments of God (Prov. 4:11) and is characterized by prudence (Prov. 8:12), discernment (Prov. 14:8), and humility (Prov. 10:8). It is the driving force for a life of obedience, restraint, faithful stewardship, and all that is the antithesis of the corruptions perpetrated by fleshly passions.

Fairness

Among major themes connecting animal spirits to financial crises, fairness and confidence (or the lack of it) are of particular prominence. Fairness is the fundamental ethical requirement of financial markets. Fairness concerns the comparative treatment of persons in relation to some rule, agreement, or recognized expectation.[30] Actual or perceived unfair conditions (unlevel playing fields) or unfair trading practices (fraud and manipulation) compromise trust, discourage market participation, and contribute to volatile trading.[31] Since fairness is driven by perceived reality and passionate belief, it is particularly vulnerable to exploitation in financial assets where the true worth is hard to ascertain given the complex nature of modern enterprises. This type of information asymmetry breeds moral hazard and outright scandalous behaviors, which tend to increase in euphoric periods when there is an apparent increase in the reward-risk ratio. The recent global financial crisis, for example, is often labeled a crisis of ethics.

. . . the wisdom that can solve the problems of human weaknesses must be the wisdom that applies divine truths to the human experience.

Legislative justice and ethics education have often been considered the first line of defense against unfair practices that induce social harm. While laws and ethical standards constrain outward behavior, their limit stems from the rational response by transgressors to reward-risk tradeoffs when they are hijacked by passions such as greed, fear, pride, and anger.

According to Scripture, justice and fairness are manifestations of God's moral excellence, and God's righteous character calls for believers to fulfill their sanctification by becoming righteous or just in actual moral acts. From a Christian perspective, the concept of rights is central to justice. In addition, one person's right becomes another's duty. Therefore, the extension of a subprime mortgage to an eager home buyer when the agent or lender believes the transaction would likely bring financial ruin or undue hardship to the borrower is immoral. Scripture reminds believers of their accountability as safekeeper of God's moral justice in all spheres of human activity, but especially in the realm of commerce.[32]

Instead of reacting to laws and ethics that prescribe the norms of earthly conducts, the redeemed believer pursuing a Spirit-filled life would live by spiritual norms that call for the proactive, continual renewal of their minds (Rom. 12:2). Godly wisdom complements the standard of righteousness with the laws of humility, contentment, and forgiveness, laws that are so clearly borne out in the Golden Rule (Matt. 7:12) and in Jesus' parables (such as the parable of the unmerciful servant in Matt. 18:21-35 and the parable of the workers in the vineyard in Matt. 20:1-16). The result is not a justice maintained by suppressing an impassioned drive to gratify the self but, rather, a liberated justice enabled by the insatiable desire to please the Holy Spirit. Such forms of fairness transcend legal and ethical norms.

Confidence

Confidence is the foundation on which healthy and prosperous markets are built. The loss of confidence, working through its natural conduits of fear and panic, has frozen up credit markets, precipitated business downturns, and prevented economic recoveries. Economic historians Charles Kindleberger and Robert Aliber summarize it this way: "*Causa remota* of any crisis is the expansion of credit and speculation, while *causa proxima* is some incident that saps the confidence of the system and induces investors to sell."[33] The change in the mindsets of investors from confidence to pessimism is the predominant source of instability in the credit markets.

Confidence is rational when people use available information to make predictions. Yet confidence is also trust, which, by nature, goes beyond the rational. People act according to what they trust to be true, and the ebbs and flows of economic tides speak volumes about the trust people have in the wrong things: crooks, profiteers, speculators, and things that have overblown values. To the Christian, the truth on which trust rests transcends the tangible and the shifting of fortunes, "for we walk by faith, not by sight" (2 Cor. 5:7) and "The Lord will be our confidence" (Prov. 3:26). Trust must be in the right object, and the trustworthiness of the object must be grounded in evidence that endures the test of time. Such trust breeds confidence, and confidence displaces fear. As Paul reminds Timothy in 2 Timothy 1:7: "God has not given us a spirit of fear."

Christians trust the Spirit of God who indwells each believer as a source of power, love, and self-discipline. This self-discipline engenders behaviors that exemplify faithful stewardship. In spending decisions, for example, a believer who is confident in God's provision and His call to bear witness for trust would strive to steer clear of an indulgent lifestyle. As Larry Burkett reminds us, "Our position in the Lord's kingdom will be inversely proportional to how we indulge ourselves in this lifetime."[34] John Bogle, founder of Vanguard Group, one of the world's premier investment firms, ascribes the conundrum of the most recent financial crisis to "too much focus on things, not enough focus on commitment."[35] A Christian ethic for consumption will call for frugality and contentment in our lifestyle, with the knowledge that "for where your treasure is, there will your heart be also" (Matt. 6:20-21).

Our trust in the truths and commitment of the Almighty God also brings us face to face with His demand for accountability. The Parable of the Talents (Matt. 25:14-30) reminds us that faithful stewardship in the kingdom economy means Christians should be prudent investors, not impudent speculators. Benjamin Graham, often considered the father of value investing, describes investing as seeking capital preservation coupled with a reasonable expected return, and speculation as everything else.[36] Capital preservation means retaining without loss what has been entrusted to us, and reasonable return means accruing what is expected to be sustainable economic value in a risk-justified, long-term transaction. The search for value requires a long-term commitment, whereas speculation thrives on short-term trading. Bogle laments that "When our market participants are largely investors, focused on the economics of business...(market) volatility is low. But when our markets are driven, as they are today, largely by speculators, by expectations, and by hope, greed, and fear, the inevitably counterproductive swings in the emotions of market participants…produce high volatility, and the resultant turbulence that we are now witnessing became almost inevitable."[37]

For Christians, the confidence that spawns contentment and a calmness of heart because of righteous moral acts speaks of a peace eternal. As Isaiah writes, "The work of righteousness will be peace, and the service of righteousness, quietness and confidence forever" (Isa. 32:17). In Matthew 25, Jesus offers a clear road map for Christians to live confidently in a fallen world where complacency, fear, and untrustworthiness abound. In these three parables, *The Parable of the Ten Virgins, The Parable of the Talents, and The Parable of the Sheep and the Goats,* we learned that there is judgment awaiting those who do not live a Spirit-filled life—a life that is defined by the principles of alertness, accountability, and responsibility required of the regenerated man.

Many of these same principles from Jesus' parables also undergird a majority of the policy prescriptions offered by secular analysts and bureaucrats to "rid" our future of financial crises. However, it is highly doubtful that these secular measures would have the desired, time-enduring effects since they fail to address the corrupted core of the human psyche, which requires a reformed heart and mind from submission to the Holy Spirit.

For the skeptics, they need to look no further for inspiration than the very embodiment of financial confidence itself: our currency, in which one is prominently reminded of the motto "In God We Trust."

Conclusion

In Shakespeare's famous play, *Julius Caesar*, Brutus, who masterminded Caesar's assassination and was about to engage in a historic battle, would exclaim:

> There is a tide in the affairs of men.
> Which, taken at the flood, leads on to fortune;
> Omitted, all the voyage of their life
> Is bound in shallows and in miseries.
> On such a full sea are we now afloat,
> And we must take the current when it serves,
> Or lose our ventures.

Brutus' utterance exudes a confidence that is driven by a spirit of willpower, opportunism, and optimism. If one believes he/she is onto something auspicious, there is a pervasive sense that it is time to get on the train before it leaves the station and the exceptionally profitable opportunities disappear. It eerily reminds us of the same sentiment that permeated the (animal) spirit-filled agents, be they representatives in the government, finance, or real estate industries, whose irresponsible behaviors ultimately plunged the markets and then the economies into turmoil in the most recent financial crisis. Their fate, of course, was the same as that which had befallen Brutus, who was defeated at Philippi.

Judging from the experience of the present and the recent past, the state of world economic affairs deserves nothing but a gloomy assessment of its destined path. Sovereign and household debt crises, policy gridlocks, volatility in the global financial markets, pervasiveness of financial scandals, and the wild swings in public confidence punctuate the call for more laws, regulations, and interventions by national agencies and supranational organizations. Inevitably, acknowledging the innovativeness of the rational man and the dominion of animal spirits is acknowledging the supremacy of a godly wisdom that dismisses the efficacy of human solutions.

The spiritual truths of faith, accountability, justice, and contentment are countervailing forces to the disruptive influences of animal spirits. They are never the products of legislation or self-reflection in a culture of moral relativism. Rather, they are the manifestations of a Spirit-enabled transformation of the human heart and soul. The world must be awakened to the truth that the appeal to moral or artificial restraints in the absence of the Holy Spirit's convicting and renewing power is ultimately futile. If there is one government policy that addresses this truth, however inadequately, it must be the one that honors religious liberty and the protection of free exercise of religion in all human institutions.

In reality, we recognize that the Christian worldview is under siege. For financial markets, a world that does not recognize the dominion of God will always succumb to panics and manias because its confidence is misplaced. Yet even here, exactly in the ashes of destruction and despair, Christians can magnify the impact of their witnessing. The believer, as salt and light, can effect real changes during times of economic upheaval for the glory of God. In the plethora of solutions offered for the financial crises, the Christian's voice for real reform must not be drowned out. True "confidence" can only find an anchor in a heightened awareness of moral and spiritual absolutes across the cultural landscape and a renewed sense of accountability to a higher authority who will mete out eternal judgment according to His absolute moral laws.

The Scripture leaves no doubt that, through faithful stewardship, believers can cultivate the consciousness of the divinity of their works and effect spiritual transformation around them. In defining the only reality that matters for human destiny, God uses believers as His agents to restore the whole of reality for His glory. The Holy Ghost, not the animal spirit, will be the guide for Christians as they take seriously the divine charge for building God's kingdom on earth. As the beloved cartoon character Pogo Possum would admit, "We have found the enemy, and he is us!" This admission is the real challenge for us all.

Notes

*This article was originally published in the Fall 2014 "Focus on Worldviews" issue of the Center for Christianity in Business's *Christian Business Review.*

[1] The inverse relationship between market volatility and market return has strong theoretical and empirical support in the finance literature. See, for example, Crestmont Research, *Stock Market Returns and Volatility* (2012), accessed online at: http://www.crestmontresearch.com/docs/Stock-Volatility-Return.pdf; H. Guo, "Stock Market Returns, Volatility, and Future Output," *Review—Federal Reserve Bank of St. Louis, 84*(5) (2002), 75-85; R.S. Pindyck, "Risk Aversion and Determinants of Stock Market Behavior," *Review of Economics and Statistics,* 70(2) (1988), 183-90.

[2] M.J. Pring, J.D. Turner, and T.J. Kopas, *Investing in the Second Lost Decade: A Survival Guide for Keeping Your Profits Up When the Market Is Down* (New York, NY.: McGraw Hill, 2012).

[3] J. Ferry, "Investing in the fear factor," *The Wall Street Journal* (online), (September 19, 2010).

[4] M. Farrell, "Stocks: All eyes on Greece and inflation," *CNN Money* (online), April 4, 2012.

[5] See Y. Shachmurove, "A Historical Overview of Financial Crises in the United States," *Global Finance Journal* 22(3) (2011), 217-231; C.M. Reinhart and K.S. Rogoff, *This Time Is Different: Eight Centuries of Financial Folly* (Princeton, N.J.: Princeton University Press, 2009).

[6] N.C. Logue, "Christian Virtues and Finance," *Journal of Biblical Integration in Business* (Fall 1996), 43.

[7] C. Henry, "Christianity and the Economic Crisis," *Vital Speeches of the Day*, 21(15) (1955), 1244.

[8] See, for example, C. Kindleberger and R. Aliber, *Manias, Panics, and Crashes* (Hoboken, N.J.: John Wiley & Sons, 2005); M. Bordo, "The Crisis of 2007: The Same Old Story, Only the Players Have Changed," in D. Evanoff, D. Hoelscher, and G. Kaufman (eds.), *Globalization and Systemic Risk* (Singapore: World Scientific Publishing Co., 2009), 39-50; and Reinhart & Rogoff, *This Time Is Different.*

[9] Adam Smith's idea of the "invisible hand" refers to the self-regulating nature of the marketplace when individual pursuits of self-interest eventually lead to a socially desirable outcome. According to Smith, the desire to "better our conditions" is a desire to be socially approved, and social approval is secured through good character and behavior (i.e., the ethic of reciprocity)—essentially a condition of fairness. Furthermore, these private actions, taken collectively but exercised without coordination, generate harmony and a type of spontaneous order (cf. Hayek) in the broader economy.

[10] E. Liang, "The Global Financial Crisis: Biblical Perspectives on Corporate Finance," *Journal of Biblical Integration in Business* (Fall 2010), 48-61; U.S. Financial Crisis Inquiry Commission, *The Financial Crisis Inquiry Report: Final Report of the National Commission on the Causes of the Financial and Economic Crisis in the United States.* Washington, D.C.: Government Printing Office, 2011.

[11] T.J. Sargent, "Rational Expectations," in *The Concise Encyclopedia of Economics* (Library of Economics and Liberty, 2008). Retrieved from http://www.econlib.org/library/Enc/RationalExpectations.html.

[12] It is well established that, for example, in a demonstration effect, the Smiths will borrow and spend in order to catch up with the Joneses, resulting in crippling indebtedness. In a coordination failure, depositors will rush to withdraw in fear of being shut out, forcing a liquidity crisis for the depository institution and losses for depositors falling behind.

[13] G. Loewenstein and T. O'Donoghue, *Animal Spirits: Affective and Deliberative Processes in Economic Behavior* (Cornell University Working Paper, 2004). Retrieved from http://cbdr.cmu.edu/seminar.

[14] S. Das, Traders, *Guns & Money: Knowns and Unknowns in the Dazzling World of Derivatives* (London: FT Prentice-Hall, 2006), 12.

[15] S. Basu, "The New Nemesis: Market Volatility," *Journal of Financial Service Professionals*, 66(1) (2012), 13-16.

[16] A case in point is the massive sell-off in global markets in the summer of 2011 from unfounded "rumors" about the financial soundness of French financial institutions that was floated and later retracted by a British tabloid (see D. Enrich, D., N. Bisserbe, and W. Horobin, W., "French Bank Shares Plummet Amid a Mix of Fears, Rumor," *The Wall Street Journal* (online), August 11, 2011.

[17] J.M. Keynes, *The General Theory of Employment, Interest and Money [1936]* (reprint, London: Macmillan, 2007), 161-62.

[18] G. Akerlof and R. Shiller, Animal Spirits: How Human Psychology Drives the Economy, and Why It Matters for Global Capitalism (Princeton, N.J.: Princeton University Press, 2009), 4.

[19] A. Smith, *The Theory of Moral Sentiments [1759]* (Available from the Library of Economics and Liberty. Retrieved from http://www.econlib.org/library/Smith/smMS.html), 26.

[20] *Ibid*, 29.

[21] J. Gokhale, "Animal Spirits," review of Akerlof and Shiller, *Animal Spirits. Cato Journal*, 29(3) (Fall 2009), 587-594.

[22] Akerlof and Shiller, *Animal Spirits*, 173.

[23] M.C. Jensen and W.H. Meckling, "The Nature of Man," *Journal of Applied Corporate Finance*, 7(2) (1994), 4.

[24] Regulatory arbitrage and loophole mining both refer to financial innovations or maneuvers that are designed to circumvent legal or regulatory constraints on traditional financial contracts and transactions. Common examples relate to international tax and bank risk capital regulations.

[25] M.H. Miller, *Financial Innovations and Market Volatility* (Hoboken, N.J.: John Wiley & Sons, 1992).

[26] N. Pearcey, *Total Truth* (Wheaton, IL: Crossway, 2005), 21.

[27] This is not to say that post-modernism is devoid of ethics, although post-modern ethics is not based on universal or unchanging principles. "Post-modernism rejects the idea of absolute truths, principles, and norms. It professes the validity of diversity and relativity in the definition of truths and moral virtues" (J.M. Vorster, "Christian Ethics in the Face of Secularism," *Verbum Et Ecclesia,* (*33*(2), 2012), 1-8. This cultural moral relativism makes accountability of human behavior situational since there is no universal moral reality to which one's moral judgment must correspond.

[28] W. Henley, "Life Balance in the Vortex of Changes," *Christian Business Review* (No. 1) (2012), 40-45.

[29] Henry, "Christianity and the Economic Crisis," 1244.

[30] The definition presented here is commonly referred as to procedural fairness since it concerns merely the application of an established rule or procedure and not the *substance* of the same rule or procedure. In other words, the rule (procedure) itself may be unfair or immoral even though it is *fairly* applied. The substantive fairness issue is a more contestable topic and is not discussed here. For more on this see E. Heath, "Fairness in Financial Markets," in J.R. Boatright, (ed)., *Finance Ethics, Critical Issues in Theory and Practice* (Hoboken, N.J.: John Wiley & Sons, 2010), 163-178.

[31] Boatright (ed.), *Finance Ethics.*

[32] See, for examples, passages in Isa. 33:15, Prov. 16:11 in the OT and Col. 4:1 and Heb. 6:10 in the NT.

[33] Kindleberger and Aliber, *Manias, Panics, and Crashes,* 104.

[34] L. Burkett, *Business by the Book: The Complete Guide of Biblical Principles for the Workplace* (Nashville, TN.: Thomas Nelson, 1998), 43.

[35] J. Bogle, *Enough: True Measures of Money, Business, and Life* (Hoboken, NJ.: John Wiley & Sons, 2009), 183.

[36] B. Graham, *The Intelligent Investor* (New York, NY: Harper Business, 2005).

[37] J. Bogle, *Enough*, 52.

8

The Fruit of the Spirit: Application to Performance Management

By Al Erisman & Denise Daniels

THERE IS A BIG DIFFERENCE between legal compliance and ethical performance. For legal compliance, the question centers on "going over the line." For too many, the focus is on how close one can get to the line without crossing it. Ethical performance, by contrast, focuses on doing good, which is a great deal different from avoiding doing bad. Pushing close to the line seemed to be at the heart of the Enron problem (see Enron box) and may be a factor in other crises as well.

Enron: The Slippery Slope of Moral Torpidity

In the Fall of 2001, Enron business practices were being audited by Arthur Andersen. Such audits are not simply black and white but require judgment and a great deal of wisdom. But as the word started to get out about what was going on, Andersen's auditor started shredding documents, and the world came tumbling down.

According to Bob Wright, a former Andersen executive, "I don't think even Dave Duncan, the partner in charge of the Enron account–the one who shredded the documents–one day said, "I'm going to help Enron cheat." I think the reason he did it was the incredible pressure there is on any world-class organization to be the best all the time. Then you have a client who's beating on you: 'Why can't we do this?' And Enron wasn't in there alone. There were attorneys, investment bankers, Enron management, beating on this guy who's probably trying to slow things down. Maybe I'm giving him too much credit, but I don't think so. I think it's one small piece at a time, and then you look back after two or three years and think, 'Oh my gosh, what did I do?'"[1]

Another reason simply following the letter of the law leads to trouble is rooted in the nature of the law. Laws generally look backward, fixing past problems through regulation. In times of great change, such as dealing with a business world transformed by technology and globalization, there will continue to be many situations where there is no law in place to set the mark for what is right. Ethical performance focuses on appropriate actions where the law is silent (see Don Flow box.)

Don Flow: The Heart of Ethical Leadership

Don Flow has built a business of 32 auto dealerships in North Carolina and Virginia and has established a strong ethical foundation with a set of values and practices that are exemplary. It is one thing to have such an intent, but another thing to make it real throughout the 800 people in the organization. Flow Automotive has done this through careful hiring and promotion practices that go beyond simply achieving compliance with the guidelines. Here is the way Don put it:

"I want to be careful saying all 800 believe the way I do. We think about different levels of commitment. At the bottom is Noncompliance. The next level up we call Grudging Compliance. That is, if somebody's staring at you, you'll do it; if they're not staring at you, you're not going to do it. Neither of these will work. Sometimes we let a person in the Grudging Compliance group stay for a little while. But our culture is strong enough that Noncompliance doesn't work at all. His or her peers will say, "This is not how we do business here." They either leave or are fired."

The next category is Genuine Compliance, where motivation is more external. These people say, "I really like the people I work with here. They pay well, they treat you well, if this is what you have to do to be successful here, I'll do it." We call those "good soldiers." We can't have them in positions of leadership. Over time, they may begin to see and believe, but they don't move up if they haven't made it internal.

The next level we call Enrollment. These folks believe and live it out themselves. They can't imagine not working this way. We're very careful that our significant positions of leadership are staffed only by folks in the highest category. Even a very high producer will not be in a significant position of leadership without this internalized understanding of how we operate.[2]

The challenge of ethical performance management is evident in the myriad of ethical failures in business, from Enron, to mortgage and investment banks to British Petroleum. Yet managing for ethics is challenging. Failures and shortcomings are more difficult to "pin down" before they become something big. Discussions are often more subjective. What is the basis for having a conversation about ethics beyond compliance?

We believe the nine manifestations of the fruit of the Spirit provide a great foundation for this discussion:

> But the fruit of the Spirit is love, joy, peace, patience, kindness, generosity, faithfulness, gentleness, self-control; against such there is no law.
> (Gal. 5:22-23 NASB)

Each attribute creates the opportunity for a discussion that would get at the root of ethical challenges. For an organization managed and run with an explicitly Christian identity, the appeal can be made to the biblical foundation. Individual Christians can also use these as a check on their own performance. But even in a secular organization, these nine characteristics can become a topic for discussion related to ethical performance without explicit reference to this biblical text. This may provide the start of a more explicit ethical performance assessment.

In this research, we asked whether these characteristics were being discussed even at an implicit level during performance evaluations. We gathered several performance evaluation instruments from businesses and non-profit organizations, reviewing them against the specific nine characteristics. We found that some of these characteristics were being carefully measured, but others were virtually ignored. In particular, faithfulness was commonly referenced and measured, while patience and self-control were rarely evaluated in performance reviews.

Background

In the performance management process, it is common to evaluate skills, behaviors, and performance outcomes. But businesses are seeing the importance of evaluating more than these for two different reasons. First, business failures, from Enron to banks and mortgage lenders, suggest that successful management is the result of much more than simply technical skills. Linkletter and Maciariello ask, "What do managers and executives value and why? If organizations are about human beings, from where do these human beings derive their values?"[3]

A growing literature is recognizing that business needs to do a better job of moving beyond technical expertise to encouraging and embracing ethical values in its employees and leaders. The second reason for considering more than skills, behaviors, or performance outcomes in the performance management process is that the values of individuals are increasingly being recognized for their role in creating a positive organizational environment and a positive experience for the customer. These values have a large impact on the productive environment in the workforce and also influence customers' perspectives of the business.

Fruit of the Spirit—Employee Characteristics

While we believe that the fruit of the Spirit has implications for the workplace, it would be somewhat surprising to find terms such as "love" or "joy" on a performance appraisal instrument. So our first task was to define these nine characteristics in ways which would make sense in an organizational context, with particular emphasis on presenting these in a way that could communicate clearly to a person who did not self-identify as a person of faith or recognize the authority of the Christian scriptures. We examined each of the nine descriptions of the fruit of the Spirit and identified ways each one might be expressed in a workplace setting.

Love

Love marks a caring and welcoming organization. In a workplace context, a person would express love by caring for others and making a strong unconditional commitment to their well-being; this attitude might manifest itself in an employee's relationships with subordinates, colleagues, bosses, suppliers, or customers. Employees who measure highly on "love" would be more likely to value interpersonal relationships compared with those who do not measure highly on love.

However, love could also be expressed by those who have minimal human interaction in their work; in such a case, love could be expressed by the extent to which the person sees their work as a means of ultimately offering value to others. In their book *Theory R Management*, Alderson and McDonnell illustrate the transformation that comes to the workplace when people are treated with love[4]. Dignity and respect come to characterize interactions with colleagues and customers. Ultimately, the organization may become known for this type of attitude, which pervades its culture. Southwest Airlines, for example, has "LUV" as its stock symbol, recognizing the importance of this attitude.

Joy

Joy is characterized by feelings of great happiness or pleasure and is infectious in providing motivation for work and inspiration for others. This is not the same as superficial excitement, whipped up in an artificial way through cheers and slogans, but the deep satisfaction of doing that which provides meaning. Many do not experience this joy, however, and there are frequent expressions of dissatisfaction from employees at every level of the organization.[5] But research shows that it doesn't have to be this way; one's work can provide more satisfaction than a day at the beach when people are engaging in activities which are perceived to well utilize their skills and talents in service to others.[6]

At least some organizations are looking for people who find joy in their work. In *The Little IKEA Dictionary* written by company founder, Ingvar Kamprad for IKEA employees, he discusses how the "Ikea Spirit" differentiates the company and is "built on our enthusiasm." According to Kamprad, "If you are not enthusiastic about your job, a third of your life goes to waste."[7]

Similarly, Dennis Bakke, the former president and CEO of the energy firm AES Corporation, discussed his company's approach to developing a joyful workplace in his book *Joy at Work*. He argues that meaningful work in which people can reason, make decisions, and be held accountable for their actions creates joy, which, in turn, can help ensure "the successful functioning of the team, community or company."[8]

Peace

Organizations which experience freedom from destructive quarrels and disagreement are experiencing peace. This is not to advocate for the absence of conflict, because new ideas often involve struggle and compromise. Framing conflict in the context of shared objectives can keep the tension healthy. When times are difficult due to periods of high pressure and significant change, people frequently experience pain. But it is how people respond to this pain that matters.

Peter Frost writes, "What turns pain into toxicity [at work] is when others respond to that pain in a harmful rather than healing way."[9] Peacemakers can enable creativity and cooperation, leading to great new ideas that benefit any organization. Employees can contribute to the peace of the workplace through avoiding gossip and supporting others, as they work toward the common good of the organization.

The Fruit of the Spirit in Action at the Workplace

Love ... marks a caring and welcoming organization.

Joy ... is the deep satisfaction of doing that which provides meaning.

Peace ... enables creativity and cooperation, leading to great new ideas that benefit any organization.

Patience ... recognizes the need to consider long-term outcomes.

Kindness ... goes beyond "by the book" behavior and recognizes the need to allow for individual circumstances.

Generosity ... leads to long and loyal relationships by leaving something in the deal for others.

Faithfulness ... keeps one's word in delivering what was promised.

Gentleness ... is humility practiced in spite of a position of power, allowing for communication and trust.

Self-Control... is necessary for a healthy workplace; otherwise, it self-destructs.

Patience

Patience is the recognition of the need to consider the long term. In our increasingly short-term world, there are too many examples of individuals looking for shortcuts, pursuing short- term gain at the expense of longer-term outcomes, or simply leaving at the first sign of difficulty.

In a study of 400 executives, 80 percent said they would decrease spending on long-term priorities in order to meet short-term goals.[10] Bankers and borrowers pursued short-term gains with subprime mortgages and real estate speculation, leading to far-reaching economic problems for the world.

In contrast, after experiencing production failures during 2009 and 2010, the leadership of Toyota acknowledged that their focus on speed had contributed to the problems and made the decision to add time to the planning and design process of new vehicles.[11] Our world of work is crying out for those who will restore patience to the workplace.

Kindness

Kindness stands out when it is offered at work, and much of the research on organizational citizenship behaviors and extra-role behaviors reflects this concept: A colleague recognizes a person who is struggling and offers a hand or someone to talk with; a boss sees an employee who is dealing with a difficult personal situation (a divorce, a sick child) and cuts some slack for a period of time.

People extending kindness are not characterized by always "going by the book" but recognize the need to allow for individual circumstances. "Kindness may not have yet caught on within business, but there is plenty of evidence that it is a key component of our evolutionary heritage, and instrumental in cooperative, collective behavior."[12]

Generosity

The habit of giving freely, without expecting anything in return would seem to be at odds with the profit maximization goal of most businesses as well as to the task of career advancement. But when everyone is simply looking out for their own interests, the cut-throat environment stifles collaboration and creativity.

Max DePree, long-time CEO of Herman Miller, wrote, "The first responsibility of a leader is to define reality. The last is to say thank you. In between, the leader is a servant."[13] Some businesses (e.g., Nordstrom, Costco) have demonstrated that generous return policies can actually improve the bottom line. They seek the win/win, recognizing that leaving something in the deal for others may be the best path to a long and loyal relationship. Generosity can permeate an organization when it starts with the leader, but it can have a supportive impact no matter where it is practiced.

Faithfulness

Faithfulness is demonstrated by sticking with the task to completion, keeping one's word in delivering what was promised, or simply showing up even when you don't feel like it. It is often not as glamorous as laying out a vision, but it is vital to any kind of work.

Raffoni notes that "Strategic planning gets all the cachet and all the ink, but the most creative, visionary strategic planning is useless if it isn't translated into action."[14] This topic was further developed in the book *Execution*: "If you don't know how to execute, the whole of your effort as a leader will always be less than the sum of its parts."[15] The authors define execution as "[the] systematic process of rigorously discussing hows and whats, questioning, and tenaciously following through, ensuring accountability."[16] Faithful commitment is the key to producing results.

Gentleness

Gentleness is characterized by true humility that does not consider itself too good or too exalted. It is best seen in the hard conversations at work, such as during a performance review or a necessary termination. It may be seen in the way a teacher challenges a student. These tough conversations are done with a sense of humility in spite of a position of power, allowing for communication and trust and avoiding the degradation of the individual.

If gentleness is not exhibited in the workplace, long-lasting loyalty and trust are not developed and change is impeded. In Jim Collins' classic study of exceptional companies, he identified the characteristics of Level 5 leaders as those with "a paradoxical blend of personal humility and professional will."[17] These exceptional leaders exhibited gentleness—but not weakness—in their interactions with others.

Self-Control

Self-control is the ability to control one's emotions, behavior, and desires, and is required in the face of temptations to cut a corner, bend a rule, or act in an outright dishonest way—particularly when there is the significant opportunity for gain. Executives worth hundreds of millions of dollars are now in prison because of the lack of self-control. And this is not restricted to top-level executives or politicians. The person at the lowest position in an organization may be tempted to use company resources for personal gain. Self-control is that check on each individual that is necessary for a healthy workplace. Without self-control, workplaces self-destruct.

The Study

While we have made the argument that all nine characteristics could lead to positive organizational outcomes, we were not sure whether and to what extent organizations would be concerned with them. Further, we wondered whether some characteristics might be included more often than others. We believe a good gauge of organizational values would be what they discuss in their performance appraisal process. Consequently, a pilot study was taken to examine a variety of performance appraisal instruments from a broad range of organizations to see to what extent the concepts of the fruit of the Spirit might be represented in them (see box The Methodology).

The Methodology

Performance appraisal forms from a variety of organizations were evaluated to assess the extent to which they either directly or indirectly measure the fruit of the Spirit in their employees. Those providing the instruments were assured that the name of the company and the specific instruments would be kept confidential.

A total of 16 performance appraisals from publicly traded companies (n=4), private companies (n=8), and not-for-profit organizations (n=4) were evaluated. These organizations ranged in size from a few dozen employees to large multi-nationals.

Each performance appraisal instrument was content analyzed by three trained raters to identify statements which might correspond to one of the nine characteristics of the fruit of the Spirit. For example, the item "Maintains the dignity of others" was evaluated as a reflection of love as we have defined it here.

What we do not know at this point is whether, through a factor analysis, we would find that these nine characteristics are independent or if there is a correlation between some of the nine items. Further work is called for. In addition, we didn't have enough data to make comparisons between different types of organizations. For example, it would be interesting to know if not-for-profits are more likely to evaluate certain characteristics relative to for-profit organizations, or whether publicly traded companies are less likely than privately owned companies to measure characteristics such as patience, given such an emphasis on short-term quarterly results. However, even without being able to make such comparisons, our preliminary data suggest some intriguing findings.

Results

From a sample of 16 performance appraisal instruments, we found appraisal items corresponding to each of the fruit characteristics, with some represented more frequently than others. Some instruments had more than one item which corresponded to a given fruit characteristic, and so our totals in several cases exceed 16. In a few instances, one performance appraisal item was identified as reflecting more than one fruit characteristic. For example, "Makes people feel valued" was identified as reflecting both love and kindness, and was counted twice, once in each category.

Using a frequency count, we found the following number of performance appraisal items (in parentheses), corresponding to the fruit characteristic which they reflected, across the 16 instruments: Love (17), Joy (10), Peace (40), Patience (8), Kindness (23), Generosity (46), Faithfulness (84), Gentleness (35), and Self-control (9). These data are graphed in Figure 1.

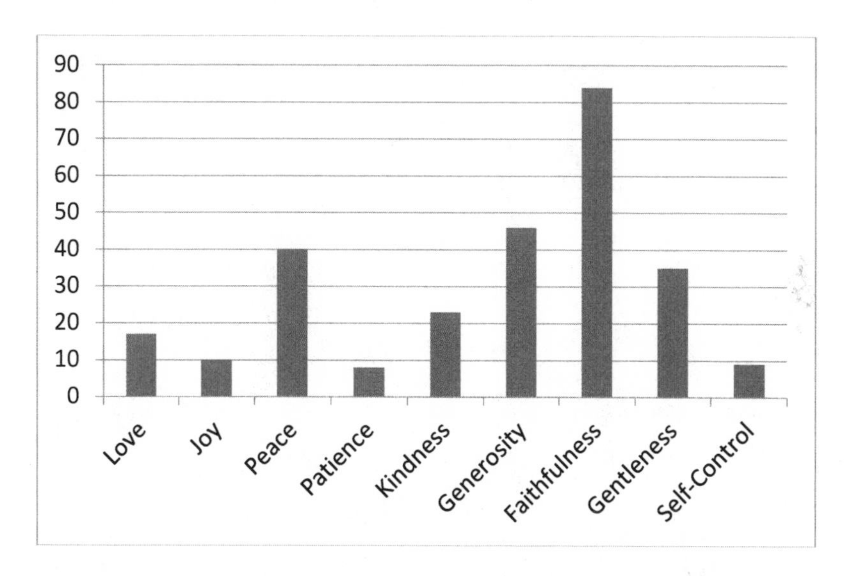

Figure 1. Frequency Count for Fruit Characteristics in Sample Appraisals

In addition to frequency count for each of the fruit characteristics, we also looked at the simple (yes/no) question of whether a given fruit characteristic was reflected in a given performance appraisal instrument. In this case, the highest score possible for any given characteristic is 16, since we had evaluated 16 performance appraisal instruments. Our data here show a similar, but not identical pattern to Figure 1; each parenthetical number indicates the number of performance appraisals which had at least one item reflecting the associated characteristic: Love (8), Joy (9), Peace (13), Patience (5), Kindness (12), Goodness (13), Faithfulness (16), Gentleness (10), and Self-control (9). These data are portrayed in Figure 2.

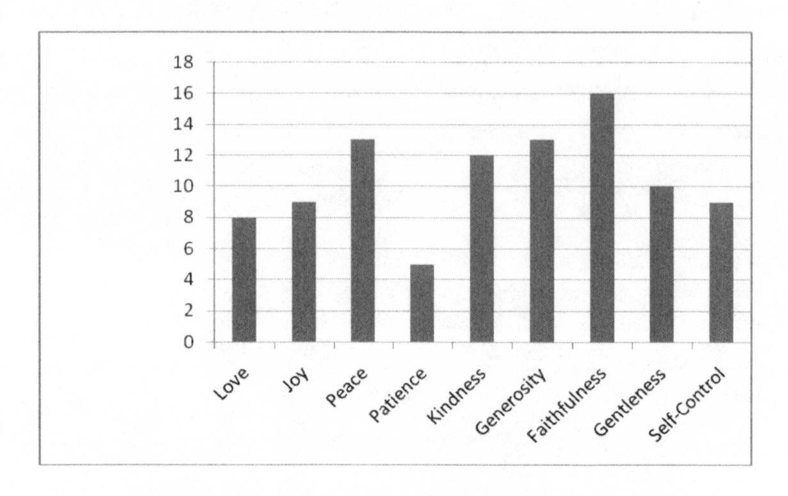

Figure 2. Number of Appraisals with an Identified Fruit Characteristic

Discussion

None of the performance appraisal instruments that we looked at took a "head on" approach to discussing attitudes in general. Yet in examining the instruments, we determined that they tended indirectly to measure many of these nine attributes of the fruit of the Spirit. Faithfulness was the one characteristic that was most frequently measured (see Figure 1). This is perhaps not surprising since faithfulness reflects the extent to which people are thorough in the performance of their responsibilities. Certainly, if nothing else, performance appraisals should reflect this attribute! But some of the more interesting findings come from what was absent from our content analysis.

Four of the characteristics we examined were relatively infrequently found on our performance appraisal instruments: love, joy, self-control, and patience. We do not find it surprising that patience was the least represented—found on less than a third of our performance appraisals—and then only reflecting a total of eight times in those appraisals in which it was mentioned. Patience simply does not seem to fit in this fast-paced, do it yesterday, globally connected business world, and it certainly does not appear to be valued if performance appraisals are any indicator of what is valued in organizations. And yet, it is not difficult to identify a lack of patience with a whole range of business problems today, from product failures to ethical failures. Perhaps this is a fruit of the Spirit characteristic that should be getting more attention.

That love, joy, and self-control are relatively underrepresented is also not very surprising. None of these terms are usually associated with business except in a negative context. Yet Alderson and McDonnell argue that relationships are really a bottom-line issue and central to any business success.[18] Joy is important for a creative and thriving workplace.[19] And many of the major business failures of the past decade point directly to a lack of self-control by their leaders. Both the attitudes that are frequently of concern to businesses according to our preliminary analysis, and those that are not, suggest the value of the application of the fruit of the Spirit to a workplace context.

Valid in the Workplace, Even for Non-Christians?

Too many Christians see a separation between their spiritual lives and their everyday lives, believing this passage in Galatians fits only on the spiritual side of life. What does this have to do with the workplace? Clearly, that is a false dichotomy. In fact, Stuart Dugan argues that when we separate our lives in terms of a sacred-secular division, this not only negatively affects our workplaces, but it also undermines our spiritual growth. We lose what we learn intellectually but do not put into practice. And since much of our waking life is spent in the workplace, this must be the place where we put important spiritual teaching into practice. Not doing so causes spiritual atrophy.

Some might argue that these nine characteristics represent what should flow from a person whose life is controlled by the Holy Spirit, and hence we would not expect to see them in a person who is not a Christian. These characteristics should flow from the leading of the Spirit and not be a guide for practice for those who are not indwelt with God's spirit. There is some truth to this statement in the context of the passage. But we would argue that every person is an image bearer of God, as the Scripture clearly teaches. As such, the characteristics reflected in the fruit of the Spirit would represent a right model for behavior for all people. Such living is clearly not possible without the empowerment of the Spirit, but such fruit represents God's intent for each person made in his image. Though attempting to live this way is not the path to salvation, living this way does resonate deeply with every human being, and we believe these characteristics can create a very positive discussion for any person in the workplace. This would seem to reflect Paul's teaching in Romans 2:15, where he argues that the Word of God is written on the hearts of every person. In talking with people in the secular workplace, we have found a resonance with the goodness of these characteristics and a place of discussion; these are not recognized as merely "religious" things.

Conclusions and Applications

The results of this study show that the characteristics of the fruit of the Spirit are present in many performance appraisals. This would seem to indicate an interest in such values and attitudes in the workplace. These attitudes and values have been linked to productivity levels, employee happiness, and overall positive organizational outcomes.

It would not be difficult to implement this work in an organization. We recommend that no attempt be made to make these measures quantitative, at least at the beginning. In a performance review, simply ask the person to identify how he or she believes they have portrayed these characteristics and prepare for a discussion about them. Encourage an employee to plan to illustrate their own demonstration of these attitudes, both in where they did these things well and where they may have missed the mark. Gaining an opportunity to have this discussion is a first step toward a more rigorous scoring that could come later.

The relative lack of some fruit of the Spirit characteristics, such as patience, joy, love, and self-control, calls for reflection on what personnel characteristics are being measured and rewarded in organizations. We would like to find more businesses which hire, promote, and develop employees with values and attitudes of love, joy, self-control, and patience and see how they differ from those which do not.

In addition, we would suggest two other areas for further research. One is to create instruments that better measure these attitudes directly and compare scores on such measures with overall job or organizational performance ratings. If found to be valid, such an instrument might prove effective in the selection process. Secondly, using the characteristics of the fruit of the Spirit might provide promise in focusing the discussion on either selection or appraisal. Discussions of these nine characteristics could be useful in the developmental process and could be used in employee orientation, training, performance appraisal, or 360 review feedback.

Knowing that these attitudes and values are important to managers and human resource departments indicates that there is a market and need for more objective measures to be created, and also for development methods aimed at improving such attitudes and values in the workplace.

Notes

*This article was originally published in the Fall 2013 "Focus on Ethics" issue of the Center for Christianity in Business's *Christian Business Review.*

[1]Al Erisman, "Bob Wright: Courage in an Ethical Crisis," *Ethix Magazine,* (January 2005), http://ethix.org/2005/02/01/courage-in-an-ethical-crisis, accessed July 5, 2013.

[2]Al Erisman, "Don Flow: Ethics at Flow Automotive," *Ethix Magazine,* (April 2004), http://ethix.org/2004/04/01/ethics-at-flow-automotive, accessed July 5, 2013).

[3]Karen Linkletter and Joseph Maciariello, Introduction to *The Drucker Difference,* edited by Craig Pearce, Joseph Maciariello, & Hideki Yamawaki (New York, NY: McGraw-Hill, 2010), 2.

[4]Wayne Alderson and Nancy Alderson McDonnell, *Theory R Management* (Nashville, TN: T. Nelson Publishers, 1994).

[5]Cf. David Batstone's *Saving the Corporate Soul— & (Who Knows?) Maybe Your Own* (San Francisco, CA: Jossey-Bass, 2003).

[6]Mihali Csikszentmihalyi, *Good Business: Leadership, Flow, and the Making of Meaning* (New York, NY: Viking, 2003).

[7]Bertil Torekull and Ingvar Kamprad, *Leading by Design: The IKEA Story* (New York, NY: HarperBusiness, 1999), 10.

[8]Dennis Bakke, *Joy at Work* (Seattle, WA: Pear Press, 2005), 85.

[9]Peter Frost, *Toxic Emotions at Work and What You Can Do About Them* (Boston, MA: Harvard Business Review Press, 2007), 12.

[10]Jonathan Wellum, Public address at the Work Research Foundation, 2006.

[11]Dan Strumpf, "Toyota Hopes to Spend More Time Developing Vehicles, Less Time Recalling Them," in the *Christian Science Monitor* (Associated Press, July 7, 2010).

[12]William Baker and Michael O'Malley, *Leading with Kindness: How Good People Consistently Get Superior Results* (AMACOM, 2008), 23.

[13]Max De Pree, *Leadership Is an Art* (New York, NY: Doubleday, 1989), 136.

[14]Melissa Raffoni, "Three Keys to Effective Execution," *Harvard Business Review Blog Network,* February 26, 2006, http://blogs.hbr.org/hmu/2008/02/three-keys-to-effective-execut.html, accessed July 8, 2013.

[15]Larry Bossidy, Ram Charan, and Charles Burck, *Execution: The Discipline of Getting Things Done* (New York, NY: Crown Business, 2009), 20.

[16]Ibid.

[17]James C. Collins, *Good to Great: Why Some Companies Make the Leap—and Others Don't* (New York, NY: HarperBusiness, 2001), 20.

[18]Alderson & McDonnell, 1994.

[19]Bakke, 2005.

9

Life Balance in the Vortex of Changes

By Wallace Henley

THE VELOCITY, SCOPE, AND MAGNITUDE of change in the contemporary world threaten the equilibrium of individuals and the institutions of their engagement, including church, family, education, government, business–workplace.

Change is the "new normal," as Peter Drucker noted at the beginning of the 21st century, when he wrote,

> Everybody has accepted by now that change is unavoidable. But that still implies that change is like death and taxes — it should be postponed as long as possible and no change would be vastly preferable. But in a period of upheaval, such as the one we are living in, change is the norm.[1]

Velocity is the speed by which the information that ignites change rushes at people in the contemporary world.[2] The accumulation of information is the fastest increasing quantity in the world.[3] Researchers at the University of California—Berkeley, examined the total production of all information channels in the world for two different years, 2000 and 2003.[4] In 2000, the total production of new information in a 12-month period amounted to 37,000 times the information housed in the Library of Congress. By 2003, the accumulation of information was growing by 66 percent per year. The total amount of scientific knowledge has been doubling every 15 years since 1900.

Information alters existing realities and also creates new phenomena. The velocity of information therefore accelerates change. The Industrial Age shows there are certain periods of mega leaps, when technologies, systems, and processes morph seemingly overnight into radically new forms. An 18th century balloon and the Wright Brothers' flying machine shared the goal of enabling humans to fly, but the airplane was a leap into a new category.

Information is a primary catalyst for change. No previous historic period has experienced the present velocity of the increase of information; therefore, the contemporary period is unique—up to this point in history. This is why change is the new normal.

The scope of upheaval is worldwide. Old values are displaced in the quest for new globally "shared" values. Individuals find the traditional belief systems that constituted the foundations of their lives shattered by the often novel alterations of the spiritual, ethical, and social landscapes. Churches that have defined and sustained core values and worldview are shaken by the contemporary transitions. The vision of families who pass revered truths across generations has been buried in the rubble of a world in turbulence.

Educational philosophies and systems seem to have been blinded in the dust of upheaval and lost their way. The principles that have secured governments have been shattered. Businesses and the workplace have rocked with the turmoil. Employees are struck with new tensions, including concerns over job security and career longevity, as well as balancing the demands of their total lives with the need to cling to their employment.

The velocity and scope of change impact people in at least three ways. First is the increasing sense of insecurity. Many people are haunted by vague, unidentifiable anxiety, manufactured within their own turbulent souls. Both the real and imagined threats of the turbulence around us drive us deeply into ourselves in the effort to fend off the gremlins of fear and anxiety. The outcome is what we experience presently: self-absorption resulting in what Harvard sociologist Pitirim Sorokin called the "sensate" stage of a culture, when feelings and emotions govern.[5] The more we view the world through the lens of our own emotions, the greater loom the threats to our security.

If we live in a state of insecurity long enough, after a while, we drift into the second phenomenon threatening life balance, insanity. This problem is at epidemic proportions, concluded E. Fuller Torrey and Judy Miller in their 2002 book, *The Invisible Plague*.[6] From 1955 into the 21st century, many medications had become available, but the number of people diagnosed with mental illness had increased six-fold![7]

Insanity is "reason used without root, or reason in the void," wrote G. K. Chesterton.[8] "The man who begins to think without the proper first principles goes mad; he begins to think at the wrong end." Cultural, societal, and national insanity occurs when people destroy their roots and forget their first principles. The velocity and scope of change in our time tears out the root-system and brings down the edifice of first principles. That's why whole societies as well as individuals lose their balance, lapse into insanity, and lose their stability.

Instability is the third impact of contemporary upheaval threatening the balance of the human psyche. The devastating destabilization of global redefinition is its impact on the foundations on which all strength and order rest. Chesterton was reflecting the theme asserted in Proverbs that the fear of the Lord is the beginning of wisdom, and yet the tremors of the present age seek to destabilize the very idea of God. This leads to the deconstruction of the concept of humans having inherent dignity because of being made in God's image. What follows is the loss of the confidence that arises from belief in a transcendent God to whom all are accountable, but also the God who is immanent in space and time, and engaged with His image-bearers and their world.

How, then, does one maintain balance amid the upheaval? The question is especially pertinent as it relates to business and the workplace. According to the United States Bureau of Labor Statistics, the average American spends 16.4 hours of every 24 working or sleeping.[9] The rest of the available hours must be allotted to many other tasks—caring for others, household activities, leisure and sports, eating and drinking. Imbalance arises as the demands of the urgent displace the essentials for equilibrium in the individual's life.

We can group these essentials into three categories:

1. the need for the "otherness" of transcendence;
2. the need for linking transcendence on the immanent scale of the self;
3. the need for a clear philosophy of time and its use.

Understood and applied properly, these three elements comprise a proverbial "three-legged stool" on which one can rest in confidence because of its balance and stability.

One of the distortions of contemporary culture is blurring the boundaries between the transcendent and the immanent. In an age of self-absorption, people increasingly worship on the horizontal level. They lose the sense of a God who is wholly other, external to themselves and their worlds. Such an attitude cuts off two legs from the stool, which becomes incapable of offering balance and rest.

"If the foundations are destroyed, what can the righteous do?" asks the Psalmist, rhetorically (Ps. 11:3 NASB). His thought is drawn immediately to transcendence, and the writer answers his own question through awareness and focus on the Most High God: "The LORD is in His holy temple; the LORD'S throne is in heaven…" (Ps. 11:4). God's throne symbolizes His serene steadiness, His immovable authority, and the potential for all under the rule and protection of that throne to enter its peace, even amid thundering upheaval. Balance begins by resting oneself on the immutability of God.

This requires linking transcendent reality with immanent experience. Thus, the Psalmist also writes,

> My soul waits in silence for God only;
> From Him is my salvation.
> He only is my rock and my salvation,
> My stronghold; I shall not be greatly shaken.
> (Ps. 62:1–2)

One of the characteristics of our time is an aversion to waiting and silence, especially in the West. Many are under compulsion to push ahead in lines, to dash under changing traffic lights, to speed toward destinations. We have been conditioned to be uncomfortable with silence in a culture that has gone from static-charged radio music to elevator music, to blaring television in doctor's and dentist's waiting rooms, to boom boxes, I-Pods, and scores of other media delivering a constancy of noise.

Our penchant for noise has come at a great cost. It has robbed us of the beauty of silence in which we can hear the "still, small voice" of God. The disappearance of silence has taken away the connection on the immanent scale of the soul with the transcendent. The loss of that connection impairs our balance, and its recovery is essential for the restoration of our personal equilibrium.

This requires an understanding of the nature of time and managing it effectively. The Greek New Testament presents two levels of time:

- *Chronos* expresses time on the existential plane. It is the ticking of the clock, the passing of the calendar. It is wholly linear, with a point of beginning and termination. It is a metric, enabling us to measure the segments of our days and lifetimes.
- *Kairos* is the "opportune time," the content of *chronos.* If linear *chronos* is the track, then *kairos* is the train, moving along the track on his spinning wheels. Therefore, *kairos* has a cyclical motion. The biblical view of time, therefore, synthesizes Western linearity with Oriental cyclical movement.

Life-balance requires that one get time in balance. There must be opportunity along the linear sequence for the recognition of the presence and impact of the *kairotic.* One must reflect and consider the events and circumstances traveling along the "tracks" and their deeper meanings, significance, lessons, and principles. This calls for a rhythm of time sequencing that allows for regular meditation, inward evaluation, and outward and upward focus.

Such balance comes as we contemplate our own nature as God's image-bearers. He is triune—Father, Son, Holy Spirit—and we are triune—spirit, soul, body. Paul prays that "the God of peace Himself sanctify you entirely; and may your spirit and soul and body be preserved complete, without blame at the coming of our Lord Jesus Christ" (1 Thess. 5:23).

Life balance requires us to engage in a rhythm that allows for inward evaluation, and outward and upward focus.

The body is that dimension of our being created for interaction with the external world, on the horizontal plane. The soul—the *psuche,* from which we get "psyche" and its family of words—is the facet of our whole person capable of introspection and self-awareness. Our spirit is made for interaction with the transcendent Being. We are "preserved complete" when there is a balance in our personal lives between spirit, soul, and body. Imbalance occurs when we lop off "legs" from the "stool" and try to stand on the "body" alone, or cast all our weight on the "soul," or fail to link the "spirit" with the other parts of our being.

And we lose our equilibrium when we neglect the wholeness of time, expressed in the *chronos-kairos* linkage. It is the recognition of and participation in the rhythm of time that can bring our whole being into balance. "Remember the Sabbath day, to keep it holy," says the commandment. That is, there must be a specific regularity in the linear flow of our routines when we pause and engage with God, the transcendent One. We must thrust our souls outward from the self and the horizontal and open ourselves to the *kairos* of God that gives us meaning and purpose.

Ben Young says he was impacted by insights from Lauren Winner, an Orthodox Jew who became an evangelical Christian. She said that what she missed from her routine as a practicing Jew was the Sabbath observance, "a cessation from the rhythm of work and world, a time wholly set apart, and, perhaps above all, a sense that the point of *Shabbat,* the orientation of *Shabbat,* is toward God." Young agrees. Modern humanity is missing something through its loss of the Sabbath concept, and "we are missing it because we don't understand what we have lost."[10]

The promise attached to the Sabbath command is that we will find "rest" precisely because of the balance and resulting peace and confidence that comes from living in the wholeness for which God designed us. Jesus Christ freed us from a rigid conformity to the Law as the means of salvation, but He did not set aside the overarching principles God's "way" provides for healthy, balanced living.

Balancing the demands of life and work necessitates, as Chesterton said, beginning with "first principles," and that means recognizing how we are made and how we relate to the time God has given us.

Notes

[1] Peter Drucker, *Management Challenges for the 21st Century,* New York: Harper Business, 1999.

[2]Material used here relating to velocity, scope, and magnitude is drawn from the author's book: Wallace Henley, *Globequake: Living in the Unshakeable Kingdom while the world falls apart,* Nashville: Thomas Nelson, July, 2012.

[3] "The Speed of Information," *The Technium,* 2006. Retrieved from: http://www.kk.org/thetechnium/archives/2006/02/the_speed_of_in.php.

[4] *Ibid.*

[5] Pitirim Sorokin, *Social and Cultural Dynamics,* Transaction Publishers, 1985, 622–623.

[6] E. Torrey Fuller and Judy Miller, *The Invisible Plague,* New Brunswick, NJ: Rutgers University Press, 2002.

[7] "Anatomy of an Epidemic," Robert Whitaker, *Ethical Human Psychology and Psychiatry,* Vol. 7, Number 1, Spring, 2005.

[8] G.K. Chesterton, *Orthodoxy.* Published originally in 1908, with numerous subsequent editions.

[9] "Time use on an average workday for employed persons ages 25 to 54 with children." Retrieved from http://www.bls.gov/tus/charts.

[10] Ben Young & Dr. Samuel Adams, *Out of Control: Finding Peace for the Physically Exhausted and Spiritually Strung Out,* Nashville: Nelson Books/Thomas Nelson, 2006, 65.

10

Communication Technologies and Interpersonal Relationships: Some Considerations from Theology

By Randy Beavers, Denise Daniels, Al Erisman, and Don Lee

FOR CENTURIES OF HUMAN HISTORY, relationships have been rooted in presence. What a person said and did in a variety of situations were factors in shaping a relationship. A person was brave, bold, kind, caring, or collaborative (or the opposite of these) and this was evident in what that person said and did in the presence of others. For the most part, relationships occurred face-to-face. Historically, technology supplemented face-to-face relationships, for example, through letter writing. Recently, technological advancement has enabled new methods of interpersonal interactions, changing our understanding of what a relationship is and how we engage in it. For example, instead of requiring two people to be in the same place at the same time in order to interact, technology allows people to engage while in different places, or to communicate at different times. It has opened up opportunities for many more relationships, allowed global teams to work together from different locations, allowed access to new talent or new customers, and created unprecedented collaboration across the world. These changes provide positive opportunities for us to create and extend relationships, but they also create significant challenges. Because technology is changing at such a rapid pace, we are often unaware of the ways in which it affects us and our interactions with others.

Assuming that relationships and technology are both under God's dominion, it is particularly important for Christians to be attentive to how technology might impact our view of and communication with others, as well as how we might utilize technology to be aligned with God's purposes for us. We need to ask how technology influences relationships and to what extent these impacts facilitate or hinder God's intent.

Technology is "the totality of methods rationally arrived at and having absolute efficiency in every field of human endeavor," according to Jacques Ellul.[1] Often, though not always, it is associated with the application of science to achieve some practical end. The term "technology" has often been used to refer to information technology or digital devices, but the subject is much bigger. There are implications of technology that we should be aware of if we want to understand the role of technology in our lives. We will highlight two: one that applies to technology generally, and one specific to information technology.

First, technology has unintended consequences.[2] A technology created to solve one problem might later solve a different problem. The automated teller machine (ATM) was created to shorten the lines inside a bank, but it ultimately resulted in the advent of 24-hour banking when it was moved outside the bank building. Conversely, a technology used to solve one problem can create a different problem. The automobile not only improved the ability to move from place to place in a timely way but also introduced pollution, traffic accidents, and so forth. The same technology used for good (driving to see friends) can be used for evil (bank robber's getaway car), and various technologies can be combined to create something completely new and altogether un-envisioned by their creators. For example, the computer chip, a modem, the internet, and security technologies are combined to make online commerce possible. While we will never eliminate unintended consequences, we can evaluate what might go wrong in the use of technology and seek to mitigate against the potential misuse of the technology. Certainly, after the evidence of misuse is recognized, we can seek to manage it. For example, debating something via email may lead to a divergence of understanding, and a face-to-face conversation may be better to resolve a misunderstanding.

Second, information technology, in particular, has a very high pace of change. Moore's law says that every two years, the number of transistors per square inch will double.[3] Roughly interpreted, this means that every two years, any device dominated in cost by the transistor will either drop by a factor of two for the same performance or double in performance for the same price. When combined with the unintended consequences discussed above, this means that completely new ways of doing things can appear almost overnight. This has two important consequences: 1) Since people absorb change at different rates, some people will quickly get on board the new way of doing things, while others (for reasons of priority, cost, or learning) are left behind. This suggests we should make relationships a significant factor in deciding whether to use a given technology. Rather than use video conferencing because we can, we should ask what might be missing in how we relate to each other and seek other solutions to fill in and 2) Each new opportunity opens the possibility for exploitation that can be used by those with nefarious intent. There is a time lag, sometimes significant, between when someone discovers a way to exploit the technology and when others uncover what is going on. Toxic mortgage-backed derivatives and the polluting effect of Volkswagen diesel engines are illustrations of this.

While the unintended consequences and high pace of change associated with technology will change the nature and types of our relationships, Christian theology provides a lens through which we can evaluate these changes. In this paper, we outline some theological principles that undergird our understanding of what God intends for relationships, as well as ways that our relationships are either consistent or inconsistent with God's intentions. We then discuss ways in which communication technology can amplify both positive and negative aspects of relationships, providing examples from the workplace. Finally, we summarize our conclusions about ways that Christians could think about and engage with technology, and we discuss some areas where future research would be useful.

Theological Values Undergirding Relationships and Technology

Before we turn our attention to a discussion of relationships and the ways in which technology can influence them, we need to start with an overview of some theological principles that help us understand God's intent for both technology and relationships. While many Christian scriptures have implications for technology and relationships, in this section, we focus on three critical principles from the creation narrative, as well as some additional concepts emphasized in the New Testament.[4]

Implications from Creation

First, we learn from the opening chapters of Genesis that humans are created in God's image: "[In] the image of God he created them. Male and female he created them."[5] While this can mean many things, most agree that it places particular worth on humankind. Thus, in relationships, we should seek to recognize the particular worth—the *imago Dei*—of another person.

A second theological principle derived from the creation narrative with implications for relationships is that each member of the Godhead is in *relationship* with the other members of the Trinity. We see this allusion when God says, "Let us make man in our image..."[6] A foundational view of God in Scripture is one of being in relationship—we see the three persons of the Trinity interacting and communing with one another. So we too are designed to be in relationship with God and with each other. When God sees that Adam is alone since no animal was like him, God says, "It is not good"[7] and creates for Adam a partner in Eve. To the extent that technology allows us to communicate better and to develop and maintain relationships, it may be one avenue through which we can live out God's purposes for humanity.

The third theological principle is derived from the Creation Mandate (sometimes referred to as the Cultural Mandate), where God tells Adam and Eve to "be fruitful and increase in number; fill the earth and subdue it. Rule over the fish of the sea and the birds of the air and over every living creature that moves on the ground."[8] Later, God gives Adam the responsibility to name the animals. These commands require that humans continue the *creative activities* that God began. We are invited to use our creative energies to cultivate the raw materials of creation into something new. While there may be obvious implications of the Creation Mandate for reproduction and agricultural cultivation, many theologians have also understood it to apply to every aspect of humanity's creative impulses, from physical artifacts such as making clothes, building houses, and creating art, to organizational policies and practices, to creating government structures[9]—and yes, even creating technology. God could have created a computer tree from which we gather hardware and software; however, he instead chose to provision the world perfectly and invite us into the creative process. The human creation of technology is one of the ways in which we reflect God's design for humanity. In the same way that God's creativity produced an order that sustained human life, trees that were "pleasing to the eye and good for food,"[10] human creativity too can contribute to order, be aesthetically pleasing, and be useful in meeting human needs.

Other Biblical Implications

One result of sin in the Garden was the breaking of relationships, both between humans and God and between humans themselves. We see this clearly in Genesis 3 as Adam blames Eve and God for the sin ("that woman you gave me," he says to God). But the Bible is clear that relationships remain important, rooted in the fact that other humans are image bearers, even in the presence of sin.[11] Further, Jesus's teachings on healing broken relationships[12] and the importance of another person[13] underscore our need to prioritize the role of relationships.

We must recognize that not every aspect of our relationships or creativity will align with God's purposes. Nonetheless, it is important to see that, from the very beginning, the importance of relationships and creativity are rooted in who God created us to be. It is also important to note that as followers of Christ, we are to be agents of *reconciliation* in the world,[14] and this includes bringing reconciliation to our relationships. Because we are designed for good relationships, yet we are living in a world marred by the fall, the relationships that we build and maintain will have both healthy and unhealthy components. A vital step is not to attempt to "go it alone" as an individual. Wise counsel can be a great support to helping us overcome our own blind spots, and in Matthew 18, we are reminded that when we get stuck in a relationship issue, we should engage others. In the next section, we discuss some factors that determine the health of relationships.

Healthy and Unhealthy Relationships

What determines whether a relationship is healthy or not? This is where Christian theology can provide helpful guidance. As Scripture highlights, *humans are created in the image of God.* We are God-breathed soul inhabitors, made for life beyond the world that we know. C. S. Lewis (1941) famously said, "There are no ordinary people. You have never talked to a mere mortal. Nations, cultures, arts, civilizations—these are mortal, and their life is to ours as the life of a gnat. But it is immortals whom we joke with, work with, marry, snub and exploit."[15] Healthy interpersonal relationships are marked by a recognition that others are intrinsically and eternally valuable, regardless of what they do or do not do for us. When we view others as important simply because of who they are, rather than objectifying and viewing them as instrumental to our own ends, we both honor God and the person made in God's image.

Appropriate levels of trust also characterize healthy interpersonal relationships. This trust needs to be mutual as far as possible[16] and built on demonstrating trustworthiness. Healthy relationships are marked by a level of personal sharing and vulnerability appropriate to the particularities of the relationship. For example, sharing intimate details about oneself with a spouse or close friend who holds that information in confidence is healthy. Sharing the same information with a neighborhood acquaintance, who then shares it with others, might be quite unhealthy. In the latter case, the depth of the relationship is not commensurate with the information shared; there may be inappropriate vulnerability not supported by the reality of the relationship. In other words, there may be unfounded assumptions about trust with the acquaintance. Intimate relationships could be unhealthy in an opposite way. Being unwilling to share personal vulnerability with anyone—including close friends or family members—is a marker of low trust levels and an unhealthy relationship.

Of course, appropriate levels of trust are predicated on the trustworthiness of the two parties in a relationship. Trust is formed by a cognitive process through which we evaluate the ability, benevolence, and integrity of another in order to discern who is trustworthy.[17,18] In other words, one's trustworthiness inspires trust.[19] Note, however, that trust can be formed in an unhealthy manner in situations where there is deception, resulting in a false belief that the trustee is trustworthy. Relationships are unhealthy when beliefs about trustworthiness are distorted by lies, deception, and accusations.

Finally, *healthy relationships are reciprocal*. One side is not always giving and the other taking, but rather a back and forth characterizes the relationship. Unhealthy relationships are one-sided. One person makes assumptions about the other person in terms of their level of engagement and commitment to the relationship that are not true. This may occur when one person makes demands on the other without ever providing anything in return. It could also occur when one person assumes a level of connection or intimacy with the other that is not shared by the other.

In a business setting, healthy relationships are fundamental to the culture and performance of an organization, but the business setting itself sometimes works against healthy relationships. Due to the pressures of business, it is easy to treat another person as a means to get something done rather than a person made in the image of God. Further, in a business setting, we are often put together with people we might not choose for a relationship, requiring a stronger commitment to gain mutual understanding. Finally, technology may filter our perceptions of others, reducing them to a response, a voice, or a message, and making it more difficult to see them as a whole person. Meeting face-to-face, having meals together, and learning non-work-related things about another person brings them to life, allowing us to see others as more fully human. Exploring how trust and relationships are a part of the bigger story of organizational culture is important and has a business value.[20]

We are made in God's image, designed for relationship, and designed to create. Because of the Fall, our relationships may be either healthy or unhealthy. Healthy relationships recognize the dignity of others, are characterized by appropriate levels of trust, and reflect reciprocity. In the next section, we explore how our creative impulses have resulted in technologies that can both enhance and damage our relationships.

Impact of Technology on Relationships

Technology has an amplifying effect on interpersonal relationships. It is neither an unmitigated good nor evil, but it is powerful, and its consequences can result in good or bad outcomes. Technology can amplify the health or flaws in relationships, pushing them to become either more or less healthy. In order to explore this amplification effect, we discuss the impact of technology on four characteristics of relationships:[21] Connectivity, Closeness, Engagement, and Reciprocal Understanding.

Connectivity

First, relationships are based on *connectivity,* the level to which one can gain access and interact with another. Two or more counterparts need to be connected in order to interact and build a relationship. Through communication technology, humans can build and maintain relationships regardless of location and time, synchronously and asynchronously. Various modes of communication, such as email exchange, blogs, online forums, and texting, give us the opportunity to extend conversations and thus maintain relationships even if communication only occurs sporadically. Acquaintances can be made more quickly than before, and more acquaintances can be made than before. Social network platforms (Facebook, Instagram, Snapchat, Twitter,

LinkedIn, etc.) and virtual online communication tools (Skype, FaceTime, various video conferencing tools) have changed the way we interact, enabling us to build relationships in new and different ways.[22] Through social media technology, we can become acquainted with another in an instant by a click of the mouse or a tap on a screen. Our networks extend through our current connections, allowing us access to a constellation of others with whom we can start potential relationships. We can become acquainted with people far beyond our neighborhoods through the use of technology, something that would not have been possible without technology.

Technology can amplify the health or flaws in relationships, pushing them to become either more or less healthy.

This increase in connectivity may be positive in that it allows us to sustain relationships with friends or coworkers who are no longer in geographic proximity. This initial connection through technology often leads to face-to-face connections. One recent study showed that users of digital technology heavily frequent public spaces such as cafes, restaurants, and religious centers and, consequently, might be more likely to have offline interactions.[23] In this respect, communication technology allows us more opportunities to express our God-given design for relationship.

While many more interpersonal interactions are possible due to technology, the quality of these relationships may be diminished since technology does not provide us with any more time than we had in the past. The consequent challenges are much deeper than those in the relationships we had without technology: Do we have the time with another person to understand who that person really is beyond the transaction we are engaged in? Do we have time to build the trust and understanding of our neighbor or coworker when there are so many competing relationships? Is the relationship reciprocal, or are we simply eavesdropping on another person's life via social media? Increased connectivity may also imply a level of trust with someone else that is no longer based on our personal experience with them. Moreover, it allows those we do not know to reach us. When we receive a message from someone we do not know, how do we understand the validity and the intentions of the conveyed message? While increased connections due to communication technology allow us more opportunity for relationships, they may also diminish the extent to which we view others with dignity, lead to lack of reciprocity, and result in unfounded assumptions about trust.

Closeness

Second, *closeness* depicts the mental or physical distance between one another in an interaction. Technology might enhance the sense of closeness between two people by allowing for more frequent communication and interactions. For example, technology that provides high fidelity and allows people to interact in different places at the same time (such as Skype or FaceTime) might enhance their closeness to each other. Such interactions may cultivate trust and better allow us to see the image of God reflected in the other person. On the other hand, increased speed and the enhanced ability to reach more acquaintances through communication technology may also have negative effects on relationships. Communication technology may hinder one's dedication of time to build and maintain relationships due to the frequency of communication one is expected to make on a regular basis—for example, the volume of emails, instant messages, and posts that are expected to be replied and responded to. In addition, people may have unequal access, knowledge, and motivation to use rapidly changing technology, resulting in relational diminished closeness between users and non-users of the technology, or even isolation between the different populations (e.g., between generations, populations of social economic status, regions).

The type of technology may also affect the sense of closeness people experience. Particularly, when interactions occur at different times and in different spaces, people may not be able to catch the value-based cues that are usually transferred in same time/same place interactions, which can affect the perceived trustworthiness of the other. For example, texting, which is increasingly replacing face-to-face and telephone conversation for younger people,[24] may not convey adequate emotion or the nuance necessary for the full development of trust. In the era of social networking, one can have hundreds of "friends" and tens of thousands of second-level relationships. Nevertheless, the number of connections does not imply closeness; in fact, some data suggests that those with large numbers of connections in their social networks may actually have weaker interpersonal relationships—or less closeness—than those who have fewer connections in their social networks.[25]

Engagement

Third, there is a sense of *engagement* between counterparts in relationships. Engagement conveys the attention one gives to a communication interaction. A person may be fully engaged with all senses in a synchronous, face-to-face interaction, but less engaged in an asynchronous email communication. As anyone who has ever taught an online class knows, the level of engagement when interactions are technology-mediated can be hard to gauge. The typical indicators of engagement, such as eye contact, facial expressions, and body language, are less available. When the interaction occurs at different times, such as with email communication or via Google docs, engagement is yet harder to determine. Engagement is impacted by whether the interaction occurs synchronously or asynchronously. Issues of trust become difficult to evaluate: Are they who they say they are?

When we are less engaged with another, it becomes easier to think of them as an object rather than fully human. One of the significant implications of this objectification is that empathy and compassion toward the other are often diminished, resulting in behaviors toward them which minimize their humanity. Some evidence suggests that online interactions are more likely than face-to-face interactions to elicit interpersonal hostility.[26] On the other hand, other research indicates a positive correlation between some types of social media use (chatting and Facebook) and empathy.[27] The contrasting research findings suggest that the relationship between technology use and empathy is complex and will require more exploration before we have a clear picture of the interaction.

Ellul argues that efficiency is a core value of all technologies.[28] Businesses often focus on the efficiency and cost savings associated with technology, ignoring the longer-term effects of technology's impact on our view of human dignity, trust, and reciprocity. Healthy relationships require a commitment of time and effort to build and maintain. Because technology can make communication "quick-and-easy," it may also prevent the formation of meaningful relationships. The ease of interaction that technology provides may make the relationship more transactional rather than "covenantal." For example, technology can help us schedule more meetings and enable us to make each meeting shorter. However, this process of efficiency focuses on the tasks to be achieved, reinforcing the idea that the person with whom we are engaged is a part of the task rather than an agent in a covenantal relationship. Efficiency does not leave room for the casual conversation away from the formal agenda, where you may really be able to understand another person. The challenge is to embrace the value of technology without losing the healthy aspects of relationships that are central to our identity as image bearers of God.

Reciprocal Understanding

The extent to which there is *reciprocal understanding* is another characteristic of relationships. Misunderstanding others is always possible and can be amplified by technology. Consider the situational factors that can lead to a misunderstanding between two people: language, culture, background, and environment all play a part in building and maintaining relationships. A low level of reciprocal understanding depicts a situation where counterparts are communicating with each other but lack the understanding of the other person's world. For example, engineers may talk about the functional meaning of the various components of the product, whereas finance people might talk about the cost of the same components. A lack of appreciation for or understanding of the other's perspective might cause a misalignment in communication (not being on the same page), potentially putting the relationship between the engineers and finance people at risk. On the other hand, a high level of reciprocal understanding may depict a situation wherein relationships are built and maintained *despite* the differences of the situational context in which communication occurs.

The ease of interaction that technology provides may make the relationship more transactional rather than "covenantal."

To what extent does technology influence an understanding of the situational context? On the one hand, since the content of a message often requires context for full understanding, it is easy to see how misunderstandings can develop when context is stripped away through technologies that minimize contextual cues. It may be difficult to communicate context and develop trust without "living life together" and knowing the person beyond the message. On the other hand, technology may, in some cases, allow for more time for reflection and understanding than face-to-face or real-time interactions. When narratives need to be interpreted, elaborated, or explained, the time and space distance that technology can allow could be beneficial. In these cases, technology can help us contextualize the conversations and, thus, help us have a better understanding of the communicator's intent, increasing the trustworthiness and meaningfulness of a relationship. With more frequent communication, an individual's motivations and interpersonal style would be more evident.[29] Therefore, asynchronous communication via technology, compared to an instantaneous, physical face-to-face interaction, may give people more time to help contextualize the communication by clarifying, interpreting, and explaining their perspectives.

A better understanding of another's intentions and emotions may increase the experienced trust in the communication, which, in turn, helps build and maintain relationships. Francis Fukuyama drew this conclusion: "If people who have to work together trust one another, *doing business costs less*...By contrast, people who do not trust one another will end up cooperating only under a system of formal rules and regulations which have to be negotiated, agreed to, litigated, and enforced, sometimes by coercive means." [30] In some cases, communication technology will work against trust development, but in other cases, it can be used to enhance it.

Implications Moving Forward

Throughout history, technology has revolutionized communication and has required humankind to respond and adapt to how we move forward as a society. Examples include the printing press, telegraph, and telephone. However, "the internet and mobile phone have disrupted many of our conventional understandings of ourselves and our relationships, raising anxieties and hopes about their effects on our lives."[31] In this paper, we contribute to the conversation by including a theological perspective and combining research from communication, technology, and business. Even when we believe we have resolved how to do effective communication fostering healthy relationships, we know that a new technology will come along and challenge our framework once again. As we gain comfort with a technology, it could change our effective use.

Technology will continue to change rapidly, and we cannot expect to predict the practical consequences that may result. Nonetheless, there are theological principles that can guide us: Everyone we interact with, whether face-to-face or via technology, is made in the image of God. God desires us to have healthy relationships, marked by appropriate trust and reciprocity. Our calling to be agents of reconciliation should motivate us to continue to discover ways technology can be used to enhance and support relationships, and to avoid ways it undermines these same relationships. Four aspects of relationships are affected by technology: connectivity, closeness, engagement, and reciprocal understanding. We summarize the opportunities, challenges, and practical applications associated with each in the following table.

Principle	How Technology Can Support	How Technology Can Detract	Practical Applications
Connectivity	Extended networks allow more opportunities for interaction and relationships	Quality of each relationship may be diminished	Ensure that you have at least some reciprocal high-trust relationships
Closeness	Allows for more frequent interactions and relationships built outside of the constraints of same time/same place	There may not be enough time to build and sustain deep relationships	Get to know something about the person beyond the transaction at hand
Engagement	Efficient, cost-saving technology may enhance empathy for those we would not otherwise be able to engage	The fewer physical cues available, the higher the likelihood of viewing someone as an object	Recognize every person as someone made in God's image
Reciprocal Understanding	Allows for more time to reflect and understand a situation than in a real-time interaction	Misunderstandings arise when the appropriate context is missing	Give grace and understanding to both parties when disputes arise

We have seen that technology opens up many types of communication that can enhance or hurt relationships. A common danger in practice is to make simplistic rules about using or not using technology in communication. Consider the following rule: "Never email a colleague from your office, but rather walk down the hall and talk with them." If the purpose of the communication is to solve a misunderstanding, that may make sense. If the purpose is to communicate the time of next week's meeting, the interruption from talking with a colleague would be an intrusion for both of you. Thus, it is important to think carefully about the nature of the communication and use the technology that works best for the communication at hand. Rather than hard and fast rules regarding technology, we need to utilize our God-given and Holy Spirit-enabled conscience to contribute to human flourishing. The best of these decisions are not just made individually, or even "between me and God," but rather in community. This helps us get beyond our own self-justification and lack of self-awareness.

In an earlier era, Forrester and Drexler[32] introduced a way of using the various modes of communication for the effective performance of a team, focusing on face-to-face communication for trust building, using same time/different place tools for the clarification of goals and objectives, and finally doing individual work with updates communicated through asynchronous communication. As technologies become more capable, each needs to be examined for its ability to support the different motivations for communication, and used appropriately. For example, could we effectively build trust through a holographic discussion or a video chat session, or does trust require physical presence with someone? In addition, the cost of interaction in a relationship must be considered. Working with a colleague on the other side of the world, we might know that face-to-face would be desirable, but travel costs may make it prohibitive.

Future Directions

There are many considerations we have not covered or only hinted at in this paper. Throughout the preceding sections, we have referenced relationships primarily between two individuals. But we also have relationships with non-human entities, including with our pets, with inanimate objects (e.g., cell phones, Roomba vacuums), with companies, and with artificial intelligence (e.g., Siri or Alexa). What principles should guide our interactions in such non-interpersonal relationships? This may become increasingly important as technology increasingly blurs the line between objects and people.

We have not discussed the ways in which organizational contexts might shape the impact of technology on relationships. For example, the position someone has in an organizational hierarchy might make the use of technology more or less appropriate in their interactions with others. Similarly, the role of the individual with whom you are interacting (e.g., customer, supplier, or community member) may also influence the type of technology that is appropriate, or the extent to which it ought to be used. We are not aware of research that has examined the faith commitments of those in organizational leadership and the extent to which such values influence the decisions that are made about using technology. For example, are Christians any more likely than others to draw on theological principles in considering how to use technology? Future studies may well add value to the discussion of the impact of technology on relationships by considering various and nuanced organizational contexts.

Finally, technology may influence individuals in many ways, which we have not discussed. For example, empirical research has demonstrated the impact of "screens" on children's brain development, and many questions have been raised about the potentially addictive nature of some technologies. Should there be limits associated with our use of some technology? Does this depend on age, gender, personality, etc.? Does the Scriptural mandate for Sabbath apply to our use of technology? That is, if technology is a tool that helps us to work, then limiting its use one day per week would be consistent with the concept of Sabbath keeping.[33] Is there a difference between productive and consumptive use of technology in terms of its impact on the individual? Does the way in which a technology is being used have a bearing on its value? If so, are there criteria that can guide our assessment of it and decision-making about its use?

Overall, we hope that our discussion of how technology influences relationships and how theological principles can guide our evaluation of these influences might provide helpful guidance to those in organizational settings who must make decisions about using technology. We also recognize that we still do not know many things about technology and how it might influence relationships. It is our hope that future work can expand our understanding of the interaction between technology and relationships in a world of rapid and constant change.

Notes

*This article was originally published in the Fall 2018 "Focus on Technology" issue of the Center for Christianity in Business's *Christian Business Review.*

[1] Jacques Ellul, *The Technological Society,* tr. John Wilkinson (New York: Knopf Doubleday, Vintage Books, 1964). Ellul made the distinction between technique (using the stated definition) and technology (which he defined as the study of technique), but for our purposes, we will use technology for both.

[2] Edward Tenner, *Why Things Bite Back: Technology and the Revenge of Unintended Consequences* (New York: Knopf Doubleday, 1996). Tenner more fully develops the case for the unintended consequences of technology.

[3] Mike Golio, "Fifty Years of Moore's Law," *Proceedings of the IEE* (103(10), October, 2015), 1932–1937.

[4] For a more thorough discussion of theological values undergirding relationships, see Denise Daniels & Al Erisman, "Relationships at Work," presented at the Christian Business Faculty Association annual meeting, October 19–21, 2017, San Diego, CA.

[5] Genesis 1:27

[6] Genesis 1:26

[7] Genesis 2:18–25

[8] Genesis 1:28

[9] See Andy Crouch, *Culture Making: Recovering Our Creative Calling* (Westmont, IL.: IVP, 2008) for a fuller description of the implications of the Cultural Mandate.

[10] Genesis 2:9

[11] Genesis 9:6 and James 3:9

[12] Matthew 18

[13] Matthew 18:6, Luke 17:2, Matthew 25:40

[14] 2 Corinthians 5:18, "All this is from God, who reconciled us to himself through Christ and gave us the ministry of reconciliation."

[15] C.S. Lewis, "The Weight of Glory," Sermon delivered in the Church of St Mary the Virgin, Oxford; reprinted in *Theology* (November, 1941). Retrieved from: https://www.verber.com/mark/xian/weight-of-glory.pdf

[16] Romans 12:18

[17] Mayer, Roger C., James H. Davis & F. David Schoorman, "An Integrative Model of Organizational Trust," *The Academy of Management Review* (20(3), 1995), 709-34. Accessed at http://www.jstor.org/stable/258792.

[18] J.D. Lewis & A. Weigert, "Trust as a Social Reality," *Social Forces* (63(4), 1985), 967–85.

[19] Fernando Flores & Robert C. Solomon, "Creating Trust," *Business Ethics Quarterly* (8(2), 1998), 205.

[20] Both David Gill and James Heskett make the case that trust is critical to building a healthy organizational culture and that culture ultimately influences organizational outcomes; see David W. Gill, *It's About Excellence: Building Ethically Healthy Organizations* (Executive Excellence Publishing, 2008) and James Heskett, *The Culture Cycle: How to Shape the Unseen Force that Transforms Performance*, (Upper Saddle River, NJ: Financial Times Press, 2012).

[21] Organizational communication scholars have described various characteristics of relationships, but as far as we are aware, they have not been compiled in any systematic or commonly recognized way. For example, the Fundamental Interpersonal Relationships Orientation (FIRO) is a theory and measure of an individual's desired and expressed levels of inclusion, control, and openness in relationships; see W.C. Schutz, *FIRO: A Three-Dimensional Theory of Interpersonal Behavior* (New York, NY: Holt, Rinehart, & Winston, 1958). Also, Brito et.al. describe group relationships in terms of their levels of communal sharing, authority ranking, and equality matching; see Rodrigo Brito et.al., "The Contexts and Structures of Relating to Others: How Memberships in Different Types of Groups Shape the Construction of Interpersonal Relationships," *Journal of Social and Personal Relationships* (28(3), 2010), 406-431. We are using the four characteristics of connectivity, closeness, engagement, and reciprocal understanding to describe relationships in this paper.

[22] Robert Weiss & Jennifer P. Schneider, *Closer Together, Further Apart: The Effect of Technology and the Internet on Parenting, Work, and Relationships* (Carefree, AZ: Gentle Path Press, 2014).

[23] Keith Hampton, Lauren F. Sessions, & Eun Ja Her, "Core Networks, Social Isolation, and New Media: How Internet and Mobile Phone Use is Related to Network Size and Diversity," *Information, Communication & Society* (14(1), 2011), 130–155.

[24] "Texting Becomes Most Popular Way for Young People to Stay in Touch." *The Telegraph* (December 3, 2012). Retrieved on 1/30/2018 from
http://www.telegraph.co.uk/technology/news/9718205/Texting-becomes-most-popular-way-for-young-people-to-stay-in-touch.html.

[25] Stephanie Tom Tong, Brandon Van Der Heide, Lindsey Langwell, & Joseph Walther, "Too Much of a Good Thing: The Relationship Between Number of Friends and Interpersonal Impressions on Facebook," *Journal of Computer-Mediated Communication* (13(3), 2008), 531–549.

[26] See for example, E.A. Jane, "Your a Ugly, Whorish Slut—Understanding E-bile," *Feminist Media Studies (14(4), 2012), 531–536, and "Flaming? What Flaming? The Pitfalls and Potentials of Researching Online Hostility," Ethics and Information Technology (17(1), 2015), 65–87.*

[27] Franklin M. Collins, *The Relationship between Social Media and Empathy* (Dissertation submitted to Georgia Southern University (2014)), available at https://digitalcommons.georgiasouthern.edu/etd; see also H.G.M. Vossen, & P.M. Valkenburg, "Do Social Media Foster or Curtail Adolescents' Empathy? A Longitudinal Study," *Computers in Human Behavior* (63, 2016), 118–24.

[28] *Ellul* (1964).

[29] Manuel Becerra, & Anil K. Gupta, "Perceived Trustworthiness within the Organization: The Moderating Impact of Communication Frequency on Trustor and Trustee Effects," *Organization Science* (14(1), 2003), 32–44.

[30] Francis Fukuyama, *Trust the Social Virtues and the Creation of Prosperity* (New York: Free Press, 1996), 27.

[31] Nancy Baym, *Personal Connections in the Digital Age. Digital Media and Society Series* (2nd ed.) (Cambridge, U.K.: Polity Books, 2017).

[32] Russ Forrester & Allan Drexler, "A Model for Team-Based Organization Performance." *The Academy of Management Executive* (13(3), 1999), 36–49.

[33] Margaret Diddams, Lisa Surdyk & Denise Daniels, Denise, "Rediscovering Models of Sabbath Keeping: Implications for Psychological Well-being," *Journal of Psychology and Theology* (32(1), 2004), 3–11.

11

Shalom and Moral Imagination for Business Technologists

By Jason M. Stansbury

AS CHRISTIANS STRIVE to be salt and light[1] in the organizations in which they work, they will encounter technological change that influences the form and goals of that work[2]. Although these changes are driven by scientific and engineering innovation, their influences and impacts are cultural[3], and Christians, therefore, must discern[4] whether and how such changes fulfill the cultural mandate to "fill the earth and subdue it."[5] Do these changes, in their implications for a person's relationship with herself or himself, with God, with other people, or with the natural world, contribute to the peaceful interdependence among these (i.e., shalom)[6] or do they disrupt that shalom? That is, do they qualify as "culpable shalom-breaking" or sin?[7]

I will suggest in this essay that technology can contribute positively to human life in social and economic terms, but that some of its applications are exploitative or idolatrous rather than contributory. I will then argue that Christians should strive in their stakeholder relationships for "shalom," that is, the peace between a person and God, others, themselves, and the natural world that is described in Scripture as God's will for His creation. I will next explain how some technological shifts in stakeholder relationships are consistent with that shalom and others are not. I will finally argue that moral imagination is one way Christians may realize opportunities to be salt and light[8] in the organizations in which they work, by recognizing stakeholder relationships that lack shalom and reconfiguring them so that they can enjoy such peace.

Technology and Value Creation

Every technology is invented to do something, at the very least to amuse its creator or its user. Therefore, all technologies embody their inventors' intentions;[9] in addition to unanticipated "off-label" uses, a technology does what it was invented for, to some better or worse extent. In particular, technology tends to serve the interests of one stakeholder group more reliably than it serves the interests of other stakeholders[10] because capital funds the research, development, production, and distribution of a given technology. Technologies that do not benefit capital are not funded through the development and launch cycle.

Although some technologies are developed by and for other stakeholders (as workers may create new tools or consumers may build freeware), most technologies need to earn a return on their funders' investments. In particular, this phenomenon explains the paradox of increasing the prevalence of labor-saving technologies in workplaces around the world, while hours worked and wage growth have stagnated for many workers: labor-saving technologies are not typically developed, purchased, and implemented to help workers make more money with less effort, but instead are intended to help the purchasers of that capital equipment make more money with less labor (or less-expensive labor).[11]

New technology can generate value for its owner or seller in three ways. One is by creating value for the user, as the user is able to do something heretofore difficult or impossible, or is simply able to do something faster or better. A dishwasher does something that people have done for centuries, but vastly reduces the time that people spend at it, and in many cases, does a better job. An airplane makes transcontinental travel (or even some daylong business trips to another state) possible, when the time required for these activities would have once been prohibitive.

These things have value, and that value is divided between the user, the owner, the seller, and the inventor; for instance, if I value getting from Chicago to Los Angeles at the start of March in a matter of hours rather than days more than I value $500, then I buy the ticket and take my flight. If that time savings was worth $1200 to me, then the $1200 of value created by the technology is divided into $700 of consumer surplus[12] and $500 of producer surplus[13] (assuming that the seat would be flown empty if I hadn't bought it, so selling it to me is a pure $500 gain to the airline). The airline, in turn, leased an airplane in anticipation of selling seats on it, whose value exceeded the cost of leasing and operating the airplane . . . and Boeing designed and built the airplane in anticipation of selling it for more than its all-in cost to the company. Everybody wins. So far, so good.

But there are other ways to create value for the owner or seller of a technology. One is by using the technology to appropriate more of the other party's surplus. For instance, as I surf the web and browse new winter coats, the servers hosting the pages I visit may recognize my physical location as being populated mostly by people of a certain socioeconomic status. In anticipation of my estimated greater will and ability to pay for a new coat, those servers present me with higher prices than they present to visitors from lower-income zip codes. That technology creates value for the user (i.e., the website I visit) and the seller (the developer of the software), but not for me.

Similarly, I may use OpenTable to book restaurant reservations; restaurants pay OpenTable to manage their reservations and to direct diners to them, both of which have value to the restaurant. But perhaps I use OpenTable to reserve a table right before walking into the restaurant that I was about to enter anyway, just to garner reward points in the application. I can use those points for a gift certificate in a few months. But the restaurant has directly paid OpenTable (and indirectly paid me) for something that was going to happen anyway. OpenTable and I have cooperated to exploit the restaurant.

Finally, technology may be used to generate value by creating or obscuring externalities. Factory automation raises productivity, in part, because machines do the work of some people so that the people who remain produce a more total value of goods with less labor overall. Factory automation also raises productivity by pacing the remaining people, who must keep up with the machines.

In some workplaces, people run the machines. In other workplaces, the machines run the people.[14] (This is not unique to auto-parts plants; salespeople whose work has been automated by a Customer Relationship Management software package may experience something quite similar). The people may or may not be paid any more than before the automation. They may also take risks with their own safety to keep up with the sociotechnical systems in which they work.[15]

To the extent that this cost of higher productivity (i.e., workers exerting greater uncompensated effort or taking risks with their own safety) is not borne by the owners of the newly automated organization, it is external to their system of costs and benefits, so economists call it an "externality."[16] Similarly, the replacement of help desk staff with "self-serve" technical support saves money for whatever organization once sustained the cost center of the help desk, but did so by pushing the work of resolving issues to the users.

So, there are many ways that technology can be used to generate value for its inventors, sellers, owners, and users. But not all of those ways center upon the creation of economic value; some of them rely significantly or wholly on the redistribution of economic value. And some technologies exploit users or others in ways that are subtle or that even enlist users in the exploitation of others for the benefit of a technology's inventors or owners.

Shalom for Stakeholders

What, then, should Christians do to be salt and light[17] when faced with technological changes in the workplace? I argue here that a Christian's ethical orientation should be toward shalom,[18] that is, peace with God, self, others, and creation. Such peace is not merely a lack of conflict, but rather entails a set of dispositions, actions, and relationships conducive to individual and collective thriving. Such thriving includes virtues that are familiar to many businesspeople as valuable for success in nearly any organization.

Prudence,[19] diligence,[20] thrift,[21] integrity,[22] and generosity[23] are repeatedly commended in the Wisdom literature of the Old Testament and were as valuable for the ruling and commercial classes then as they are today.[24] Shalom can be understood in part as an economic order in which the creation mandate of Genesis 1:28–30 is fulfilled by humans laboring in both toilsome and creative ways to meet their own and each other's needs through production and exchange. It even seems that market exchange and free enterprise are, in limited ways, consistent with that shalom.[25]

However, shalom is also a theme in the prophetic literature of the Old Testament,[26] where deceptive, coercive, and exploitative business practices are repeatedly condemned[27], but the inclusion of the excluded and the restoration of the fallen is also repeatedly promised.[28] This God-given order for human life is normative for all relationships, and the culpable violation of that order is sin.[29]

What are the specific requirements of shalom for business? Unfortunately, while humans can know something of God's intended order with the enlightenment of the Holy Spirit, through both the study of the created world and the study of the Scriptures, human sinfulness obscures that order in both cases.[30] Therefore, circumspection is always proper when attempting to elaborate the meaning of shalom for any domain of human life.[31] Even so, a number of practices seem consistent with biblical teaching on business practices.

. . . a Christian's ethical orientation should be toward shalom, that is, peace with God, self, others, and creation. Such peace is not merely a lack of conflict, but rather entails a set of dispositions, actions, and relationships conducive to individual and collective thriving.

In general, a business exists to serve its customers with products and services that promote human flourishing, to provide its employees with the means of livelihood through meaningful and creative work, and to provide investors with a return on their investment.[32] The first two purposes are especially consistent with the creation mandate of Genesis 1, and, therefore, ought generally to take precedence over the third purpose; while all three are good and necessary, the third is generally to be satisfied while the first two are to be maximized.[33]

Moreover, the theme of humble and caring service in the best interest of others is a consistent theme in the Gospel of Luke,[34] which contains a preponderance of the teaching on economic activity in the New Testament.[35] Jesus even spoke about,[36] and Himself demonstrates,[37] a reversal of roles in which the master serves the servants,[38] indicating that mutual service is a crucial aspect of God's intended order among people.

As products and services today are typically provided by businesses rather than furnished through home production by household laborers, it seems appropriate to extend this ethos of mutual service to today's employment relationships and supplier-customer relationships.[39]

Moreover, another theme in Luke's Gospel is declining to create patronage relationships in which one person or organization becomes a dependent client of another.[40] Patronage was widespread in the Roman empire, and savvy heads of households (or their servants entrusted with management responsibilities) sought opportunities to expand their patronage networks.[41] Client households, having become dependent upon the patronage of a more powerful household, could then be exploited for economic rents,[42] whether providing goods or services at a discount or purchasing them at a markup.

Contemporary franchisees, or firms subject to the demands of a controlling shareholder, or organizations that have a few powerful customers or suppliers, sometimes experience similar patronage relationships in which their patron demands additional purchases of slow-moving inventory, or the reduction of headcount to fund larger dividends, or renegotiations of payment terms.

Yet Jesus spoke of freeing people from patronage when He quoted from Isaiah while speaking in the synagogue at Nazareth[43] ... declined to become a patron of a Roman centurion who clearly understood that his request for the healing of his own servant would make him a client of Jesus[44] ... and instructed His disciples not to enter patron-client relationships when He sent them into the countryside[45]. Patronage does not seem to be consistent with shalom.

These principles offer some guidance for the Christian businessperson evaluating a technological innovation. As discussed in the prior section, a technology often generates economic value for its inventor or seller in one of three ways: creating value for the user, enabling the user or owner to capture more of another party's surplus in economic transactions, or imposing or obscuring externalities that shift some of the owner's or user's costs to another party. Each one can be evaluated in terms of shalom.

Evaluating Value Creation through Technology in Terms of Shalom

Creating economic value for users seems non-controversial, and in strictly economic terms, it is. However, recall that any technology embodies the values of its inventor.[46] Moreover, the designer's intentions and the values that shape them may sometimes be embodied subtly in a given technology, so that they come to be taken for granted as "the way it works" for users.[47] For instance, social media users who become accustomed to photographically documenting their joys, sorrows, outfits, and meals online for a growing audience of followers and "friends" may with little consideration start to think of those events in their lives as the basis of a competition, providing them with readily measurable status, and the social media provider with motivated and creative drivers of site traffic and advertising revenue. Users may adopt a technology for reasons that are apparent to them but come to be influenced by the underlying values of its inventors in other ways without realizing it.[48]

The values that create economic value ought to be appropriated discerningly because economic value may itself become a consideration that overwhelms all other values. This caution is familiar to many Christians, as "the love of money is a root of all kinds of evil. Some people, eager for money, have wandered from the faith and pierced themselves with many griefs."[49]

While money is clearly useful for purchasing a variety of goods and services that contribute to human wellbeing, failing to discipline the accumulation of capital with the question "how much is enough?" is the *sine qua non* of greed.[50] Yet the reduction of the range of other human goods to some quantifiable measure of utility, for which money is a convenient though rough proxy, is both the key to the power of rational management[51] and its greatest weakness.[52] That reduction allows a score to be kept, which separates winners from losers and good ideas from impractical ones; it also has the advantages of simplifying accountability and motivating both managers and the managed, and coordinating interests and incentives across a range of stakeholders who are presumed in the final accounting to simply want more capital for themselves.[53]

Yet human well-being cannot be reduced to a single, linear measure of utility[54] and attempts to manage as if it could ignore the other irreducible qualities of work done well[55] deny participants in business practices the opportunity to enact their virtues,[56] debase the relationships among people who are presumed to be only using one another,[57] and ultimately foster an unsustainable economy of appropriation and exploitation.[58] To the extent that technology fosters both efficiency and control, using it could be construed as contributing to the rationalization sketched above—that is, to the idolatry of money.

Living and working faithfully in the midst of idol worship has been a challenge for Christians since the New Testament era, and Paul's first letter to the Corinthians provides some helpful guidance.[59] The cults of the Greco-Roman pantheon permeated the civic and economic life of ancient Corinth, and gatherings of political or trade associations often occurred over meals that incorporated the ritual sacrifice of the entrée to the patron god or goddess of the group before it was served to the guests.[60] Meat sold in the marketplace or served in a pagan's private home sometimes got the same treatment.[61]

Because refusing such food was socially isolating, some Corinthian Christians sought Paul's permission to partake, on the grounds that because the pagan gods were fictional, their idols were powerless and, therefore, Christians who understood these facts could eat such food with impunity.[62] Paul instead responded that while it was true that the pagan gods were "nothing at all"[63] and "everything is permissible,"[64] "not everything is beneficial."[65] Christians ought to aspire not to greater freedom from constraints, but instead to the self-discipline that enables their witness.[66]

Partaking in food that gives the impression of syncretism can confuse fellow Christians and pagan associates alike about the loyalty of the believer to God alone.[67] Because that confusion has shown itself to be so dangerous throughout the history of God's people,[68] it falls short of the love for others and God (i.e., shalom) proper to believers.[69] Therefore, while Christians are permitted to freely consume food bought in the marketplace or served in a pagan home without concern for its unknown ritual history, if they are advised that it has a ritual history, Christians must refuse such food.[70]

Can Christians use technology in business or otherwise participate in contemporary management without subjecting themselves to idolatry? Paul's guidance recounted above is useful today. Designing, distributing, or using technology that does something that wasn't possible before, or does something better or cheaper than was possible before, would seem to be no less permissible than buying meat instead of bread at the local market. But affirming the reduction of human goods (whether virtues, relationships, or the panoply of non-economic values that stem from the range of human practices) to transactional economic value would seem to be no more permissible than acquiescence in a ritual consecration of a meal.

Whether that affirmation consists of using automated services (like self-scanners at the grocery) precisely to avoid personal interaction, or using an online intermediary to choose a hotel on the basis of price and aggregate reviews without reference to the actual content of those reviews, or using gamification ("enhancing services with (motivational) affordances in order to invoke gameful experiences and further behavioral outcomes")[71] to stoke users' competitive instincts and thereby elicit greater efforts[72], Christians should resist using technology to flatten their business and personal interactions into a series of arm'slength economic transactions. In a subsequent section, I will discuss how moral imagination can help Christians to enact shalom in these interactions instead.

Evaluating Value Appropriation through Technology in Terms of Shalom

The second general form of value creation through technology, capturing a larger share of another party's consumer or producer surplus, is more straightforwardly problematic than the paradoxical benefit and idolatry of economic value creation. Deception and extortion (i.e., coercion) are straightforward ways to capture value from another party in a transaction and are routinely condemned in Scripture.[73]

Spearphishing (i.e., sending deceptive messages to email users in order to trick them into revealing their login credentials) and ransomware (i.e., using malicious code to lock a user's computer, and providing the password only upon payment of a ransom) are obviously unethical uses of technology. But more subtly, technology enables the creation of patronage relationships: raising users' switching costs enables a technology's inventor or seller to subsequently extract economic rents from increasingly dependent users.

Limiting the interoperability of software or devices with rival technologies can induce a user to commit to a single provider's platform rather than enjoying several of them, since the hassle of working around incompatibilities or learning one's way around a new user interface or re-creating lost data that doesn't transfer can be overwhelming.

For instance, 50-page user agreements that pop up on an electronic device in the midst of a routine task are one way that such dependence is exploited, since few users will abandon an application or even stop to read the new agreement. Although the dialog box that pops up collects putatively informed consent to gather ever more of the user's personal or behavioral information (to better serve the user with relevant advertising, of course), the threat to otherwise terminate a user's access to a product or service that they are in the midst of using is clearly, if gently, coercive. Leveraging the value of a product or service to increase users' dependence and, therefore, the inventor or seller's future capability to command higher prices/more access to user data/more user tolerance of security or reliability problems/et cetera, is a means of capturing more of the value created by that product or service, that is, appropriating more of a user's consumer surplus.

Nehemiah chapter 5 describes a similar dynamic during the reconstruction of Jerusalem's wall during the reign of Artaxerxes, the king of Persia: Jews who lacked the resources to feed their families were sold food or lent money by "nobles and officials" with greater means, but at the cost of selling their daughters into slavery or turning over title to their fields and vineyards.[74] These nobles were using the value of their available grain to convert freeholding peasants into serfs, that is, becoming the patrons of those clients, the exploitative potential of which transaction was recognized and prohibited in the Mosaic Laws.[75]

Nehemiah himself took offense at this arrangement, publicly berated those responsible, and exacted a pledge both to return the appropriated assets and to refrain from any such appropriations in the future.[76] Thus, even as the means of fostering dependency have changed since the eras of Nehemiah or Luke, doing so today still seems to be inconsistent with the shalom God intends for His people.

Similarly, imposing negative externalities upon another party also seems problematic. Imposing costs upon another person without compensation is condemned in Scripture, whether by negligently exposing others to risk (i.e., digging a pit and leaving it uncovered, resulting in the death of another person's draft animal)[77] or by withholding payment from workers.[78]

Patronage, of course, increases the power of someone to leave such costs uncompensated. So technologies that shift foreseen uncompensated costs to others, as through job intensification in automated roles,[79] would seem to be inconsistent with shalom. Technologies that negligently shift unforeseen uncompensated costs to others, like information systems that increase the accessibility of sensitive information to authorized users but also to hackers, in the case of the Equifax breach,[80] would also seem to be inconsistent with shalom.

Moral Imagination

Even recognizing the violations of shalom described above can be difficult for committed Christians. Because technology embodies the values of its designers, often in a way that becomes taken for granted by its users and even the designers themselves,[81] holding alternative values does not necessarily mean that a designer, seller, or user will recognize the conflict. For Christians, this can be understood as a problem of religious incongruence: the believer's actual beliefs are not entirely coherent with each other or with the faith the believer espouses, and the believer's actions may also be inconsistent with that faith.[82]

This problem can be overcome in part through moral imagination,[83] which enables a decision-maker to recognize the moral shortcomings of the status quo and identify preferable alternatives.[84] It occurs in three stages: reproductive imagination, productive imagination, and free reflection.[85]

Reproductive imagination entails constructing a mental model of the situation at hand: what is happening, why it is happening, and the values that give it meaning. Doing this accurately and thoroughly is crucial for seeing "the realities as they actually are, not as they might have been, and not as we wish they were."[86] This stage is prompted by a "paradigm failure,"[87] in which a person becomes aware that the situation at hand poses problems that her or his set of norms and ways of seeing the problem cannot solve; what is crucial is that it makes explicit the mental models that currently are used to justify the status quo. That step especially can help Christians to realize that something about the status quo is at odds with their faith commitments.

Productive imagination then identifies alternatives: How else might the parties involved relate to each other? Why else might that happen? What other values might give those alternative relationships meaning? This stage generates practical and moral alternatives by reconfiguring elements of the reality at hand.

Finally, free reflection evaluates these alternatives by asking whether they are practically and morally appropriate to the situation, using the range of values identified in the productive imagination stage. Free reflection enables the decision-maker to identify an alternative potential reality that is both feasible and morally preferable to the status quo.[88]

Moral imagination has been studied in simulations among part-time MBA students,[89] surveys of businesspeople,[90] and case studies in the field.[91] These have revealed that an organizational culture in which ethics is important has a significant effect on employees' tendency to consider alternatives and evaluate them in ethical terms, though that effect is strongest for employees who consider ethics less important to their senses of self, while employees for whom ethics is personally important are already more likely to exercise moral imagination and, therefore, less affected by organizational culture.[92]

Moral attentiveness (a person's tendency to evaluate situations in ethical terms) tends to promote moral imagination, and this relationship is stronger for more creative employees.[93] When moral imagination is exercised by businesspeople to realistically assess the inadequacies of the status quo, conceive new configurations of stakeholder relationships, and partner with other organizations to address problems that were unsolvable under the prior status quo, they can overcome problems like sweatshops in the apparel supply chain[94] or governance, corruption, and environmental impact in petroleum production.[95]

Notwithstanding the influence of the concept of moral imagination in the business ethics literature, some readers may wonder whether the lack of Scriptural references above indicates a reliance upon "hollow and deceptive philosophy, which depends on human tradition ... rather than on Christ."[96] It is true that the origin of the concept of moral imagination described above is in the philosophy of Immanuel Kant[97] and not in the Christian tradition.

However, the concept of common grace in the Reformed tradition of Protestant Christianity highlights that out of His love for the human race and His merciful will to prevent sin and ignorance from having their full effect, God gives insight and even genius to people who do not know or acknowledge Him.[98] These insights are useful for thinking clearly and acting prudently, and even correcting Christians' own sinful errors, so it is valuable for Christians to discerningly avail themselves of those insights.[99]

That said, such discernment requires asking whether the concept of moral imagination is, at the very least, consistent with the witness of Scripture. Bruno Dyck's careful exegesis of the Gospel of Luke with respect to the theme of economic relationships[100] revealed a repeated pattern of four phases of learning and action in the "journey narrative" from Luke 9:51 to Luke 19:40, whereby the disciples came to better understand the implications of Jesus's teachings about the Kingdom of God for daily life.

This pattern was repeated three times between Luke 9:51 and Luke 13:30 before being repeated three times in reverse between Luke 14:1 and Luke 19:40. The "reverse cycles" recount "institutional change" (i.e., a shift in social norms and structures, like inviting the poor to a banquet in Luke 14), a "changed way of seeing" the situation (e.g., loving Jesus more than one's own family, also in Luke 14), an "action response," (e.g., welcoming home the prodigal son in Luke 15), and "problem recognition" (e.g., commending the shrewd manager who scattered his master's possessions by writing down his master's accounts receivable, before pointing out that one cannot love both God and money in Luke 16).[101]

The first stage in the reverse cycle, institutional change, bears some resemblance to the reproductive imagination that comprehends a technological change to existing relationships within and across workplaces. The second stage, a changed way of seeing, bears a resemblance to the productive imagination that recognizes alternative values to those reified in the status quo and envisions alternative configurations of resources and relationships. The third stage, an action response, is typically seen in the business ethics literature as an outcome of moral imagination rather than a component of it.[102]

But pairing faith with works is crucial for Christian discipleship,[103] and Dyck found in his exegetical study of Luke that acting on a changed way of seeing was crucial for the fourth stage in the reverse cycle: the Disciples' realization that the Kingdom of God differed in its values and practices even more than they had realized from the world they knew. Altogether, moral imagination bears some significant resemblance to the stages of the "reverse cycle," whereby the disciples learned to see the Kingdom of God in everyday life, though Luke's journey narrative emphasized action as a part of the learning cycle rather than as its outcome.

Moral Imagination: An Example

A Christian manager may identify an opportunity to install self-service checkouts at a chain of retail stores. Exercising reproductive imagination requires assessing the advantages and disadvantages of that opportunity, and the values underlying them.

Such automation has many advantages: reducing the store's reliance on human laborers who may commit errors in customer service, miss work, or show up late, or demand raises; attracting customers who prefer not to interact with other people during their shopping experience; and keeping greater checkout capacity available rather than having to staff up or down at peak times. The values underpinning these advantages include providing a more consistent transactional experience for the customer, reducing several aspects of operational variability, and, of course, making a return on investment from the prior two.

The disadvantages include reducing personal interaction and perhaps relationships with customers, reducing the opportunities available to low-skilled laborers, and reducing the flexibility of the checkout experience to accommodate emergent or unusual customer needs (e.g., questions, or disabilities). As inclusion of the excluded is integral to shalom,[104] this change would seem to pose some problems.

If the Christian manager were to engage in productive imagination, s/he might then consider alternatives: what if the checkout is not a barrier between the customer and the door, but instead is an opportunity to enhance the customer's experience through personalization and relationship? What if the checkout is an important opportunity for unskilled laborers to begin developing knowledge, skills, and relationships that prepare them to advance to positions of greater responsibility in the store?

After all, it is hard to match the transactional efficiency of the internet, so a bricks-and-mortar retailer may want to invest in a more compelling shopping experience rather than a more minimal one. Perhaps installing self-checkout stations but using them to handle peak times, rather than using them as the default checkout option and staffing up manual lines at peak times, would realize such goals. The manager might then engage in free reflection, to consider whether and how the shoppers, checkout clerks, and store owners are better off under such an alternative, and whether shalom is thereby better served.

Without training in product knowledge or relationship-building techniques, checkout clerks may find their jobs stultifyingly transactional, and customers may be frustrated by the store's failure to adopt self-checkout. But if checkout clerks are empowered to assist customers with idiosyncratic requests and needs, educated on product attributes and combinations so that they can converse meaningfully with customers about their purchases, and trained on techniques for recognizing whether a customer wants to chat or is in a hurry, then their experiences and the customers' would be enhanced. They would gain opportunities to exercise virtues like the love of learning or empathy and bolster their opportunities for advancement. At least some customers would build cordial or even friendly relationships with checkout clerks. Peace among people and within people would increase, and the Christian manager would thereby enjoy peace with God.

Conclusions

While the moral implications of technological change in business can be difficult to analyze, I have suggested that the biblical concept of shalom can help. In particular, while technology creates a bewildering array of foreseen and unforeseen effects on human relationships, grouping those effects into three general forms—value creation, value appropriation, and creating or obscuring externalities—makes those effects more analyzable.

Shalom highlights that the latter two forms are exploitative of others and, therefore, unbiblical, while the first form has idolatrous potential that can also violate shalom. Moral imagination can help Christians to discern the problems associated with new technological applications and identify ways to resolve them. Future research on technology and shalom in business might extend this analysis by examining problems of unforeseen consequences of technology adoption, or problems of the appropriateness of control of other people enabled by technology.

In practice, Christians striving to apply new technologies appropriately might apply moral imagination as follows: when faced with an innovation of some sort, the first challenge is to explain what it does, why it works, and why that is valuable. Because technology in business tends to serve the interests of the capital provider who pays for its development and deployment, it is important to specify how the technology creates value: does it do something that wasn't possible before, or perhaps do something familiar somehow better? Does it appropriate economic surplus from other parties, or perhaps impose negative externalities on them? What values, economic or otherwise, are shared by its users, buyers, or others?

Asking these questions facilitates reproductive imagination that makes explicit both what works about the status quo and what might be morally problematic. Next, a Christian decision-maker should engage productive imagination and imagine some alternative configurations. What other values might be prioritized besides the ones identified in the prior stage? In particular, it can be valuable to re-order stakeholders:[105] what if the technology in question were being used primarily to enhance the work lives and material sustenance of the labor force, or to provide a good or service that enables customers to thrive, and only secondarily to generate a return on capital investment?

That thought experiment can highlight opportunities to serve customers and labor, and may well also provide adequate or better investment returns. Finally, a Christian decision-maker should do some free reflection to evaluate the alternative configurations imagined in the second stage. Would they be feasible? Would they promote interdependence rather than dependence among stakeholders? Would they embody an ethos of service rather than one of being served? That is, would they promote shalom better than the status quo? Moral imagination can help the Christian businessperson to see alternatives that are more consistent with her or his beliefs, even for unfamiliar technologies.

To increase her or his capacity for moral imagination, a Christian businessperson could take several measures. First, knowledge of Scripture can help her or him to be "transformed by the renewing of [their] mind . . . [to] be able to test and approve what God's will is,"[106] enabling a better evaluation of the shalom of a technological innovation.

Second, familiarity with both the experiences of stakeholders and the implications of technologies increases one's capacity for both reproductive and productive imagination. Reading widely, meeting and conversing with a range of people, and taking opportunities to experience different parts of a business all help to develop a wider set of perspectives that can be brought to bear in either form of imagination.[107]

Finally, practicing creativity in low-stakes problem-solving, that is, generating novel solutions and evaluating them for their practicality and appropriateness, can bolster one's capability for productive imagination and free reflection on more important problems.

Altogether, while technological change poses challenges for Christians striving to live at peace with God and others, moral imagination can help such Christians to identify opportunities to reconfigure their business practices and relationships in the service of such peace, sometimes even by adopting new technologies!

Notes

*This article was originally published in the Fall 2018 "Focus on Technology" issue of the Center for Christianity in Business's *Christian Business Review.* The author would like to acknowledge the generous support of James and Judith Chambery for his research agenda.

[1] Matthew 5:13-16. Also, Bruno Dyck & Frederick A. Starke, "Looking back and looking ahead: A review of the most frequently cited Biblical texts in the first decade of the JBIB," *Journal of Biblical Integration in Business* (11, 2005), 134–153.

[2] Mark Muro, Sifan Liu, Jacob Whiton, & Siddharth Kulkarni, *Digitalization and the American Workforce* (Washington, DC: Brookings Institution Metropolitan Policy Program, 2017). Accessed June 1, 2018 at https://www.brookings.edu/wp-content/uploads/2017/11/mpp_2017nov15_digitalization_full_report.pdf.

[3] Philip Anderson & Michael L. Tushman, "Technological discontinuities and dominant designs: A cyclical model of technological change," *Administrative Science Quarterly*, (35(4), 1990), 604–633.

[4] Albert M. Wolters, *Creation Regained: Biblical Basics for a Reformational Worldview* (2nd ed.) (Grand Rapids, MI: Wm. B. Eerdmans, 2005). See especially pages 135–140.

[5] Stephen V. Monsma, *Responsible Technology: A Christian Perspective* (Grand Rapids, MI: Calvin Center for Christian Scholarship, 1986).

[6] Nicholas Wolterstorff, *Until Justice and Peace Embrace* (Grand Rapids, MI: Wm. B. Eerdmans, 1983). Also Walter Brueggemann, *Living toward a Vision: Biblical Reflections on Shalom* (Philadelphia: United Church Press, 1976).

[7] Cornelius Plantinga, *Not the Way It's Supposed to Be: A Breviary of Sin* (Grand Rapids, MI: Wm. B. Eerdmans, 1996).

[8] Matthew 5:13-16. Also Dyck & Starke.

[9] Monsma.

[10] Harry Braverman, *Labor and Monopoly Capital* (New York, NY.: Monthly Review Press, 1974).

[11] *Ibid.*

[12] Hal Varian, *Intermediate Microeconomics: A Modern Approach (3rd ed.)* (New York, NY.: W. W. Norton, 1993).

[13] *Ibid.*

[14] David Hounshell, *From the American System to Mass Production, 1800-1932: The Development of Manufacturing Technology in the United States* (Baltimore, MD.: Johns Hopkins University Press, 1984).

[15] Peter Waldman, "Inside Alabama's auto jobs boom: Cheap wages, little training, crushed limbs," *Bloomberg Businessweek* (March 23,

2017). Accessed June 2, 2018 at https://www.bloomberg.com/news/features/2017-03-23/inside-alabama-s-auto-jobs-boom-cheap-wages-little-training-crushed-limbs.

[16] Varian.

[17] Matthew 5:13-16. Also Dyck & Starke.

[18] Wolterstorff.

[19] E.g., Proverbs 4, Proverbs 8

[20] E.g., Proverbs 6:9-11, Proverbs 10:4-5, Proverbs 10:26

[21] E.g., Proverbs 6:6-8

[22] E.g., Proverbs 10:9, Proverbs 11:1

[23] E.g., Proverbs 11:16-17; Proverbs 11:25

[24] Brueggemann.

[25] John Bolt, *Economic shalom: A Reformed primer on faith, work, and human flourishing* (Grand Rapids, MI.: Christian's Library Press, 2013). Also, for instance, Proverbs 3.

[26] Brueggemann.

[27] E.g., Isaiah 58; Micah 6:9-16; Amos 2 and 4

[28] E.g., Isaiah 58; Amos 9:11-15; Micah 7:11–20

[29] Plantinga.

[30] Bolt.

[31] *Ibid.*

[32] Jeff Van Duzer, *Why business matters to God (and what still needs to be fixed)* (Downers Grove, IL: IVP Academic, 2010).

[33] *Ibid.*

[34] E.g., Luke 7:1-10; Luke 12:35–38; Luke 12:41–48; Luke 22:24–30, as noted in Bruno Dyck, *Management and the Gospel: Luke's radical message for the first and twenty-first centuries* (New York, NY.: Palgrave Macmillan, 2013).

[35] *Ibid.*

[36] Luke 12:37

[37] Luke 22:27; John 13:1-16

[38] See Dyck.

[39] See Dyck, and also Van Duzer.

[40] Dyck.

[41] *Ibid.*

[42] *Ibid.*

[43] Luke 4:18-19

[44] Luke 7:1-10

[45] Luke 10:1-20. This and the two prior passages in Luke are discussed in Dyck.

[46] Monsma.

[47] Perrow.

[48] Monsma.

[49] 1 Timothy 6:10 (NIV)

[50] Ron Blue & Karen Guess, *Never Enough? 3 Keys to Financial Contentment* (Nashville, TN: B&H Publishing Group, 2017). See also Mark Cheffers & Michael Pakaluk, *Understanding accounting ethics* (2nd ed.) (Sutton, MA.: Allen David Press, 2007). Also See Dyck, and Rebecca Konyndyk DeYoung, *Glittering Vices: A New Look at the Seven Deadly Sins and Their Remedies* (Grand Rapids, MI: Brazos Press, 2009).

[51] Michael Jensen, "Value maximization, stakeholder theory, and the corporate objective function," *Business Ethics Quarterly* (12(2), 2002), 235–256.

[52] Gerald F. Davis, *Managed by the Markets: How Finance Reshaped America* (New York, NY.: Oxford University Press, 2009). See also Sumantra Ghoshal, "Bad management theories are destroying good management practices," *Academy of Management Learning & Education* (4(1), 2005), 75-91, and Alasdair MacIntyre, *After virtue* (3rd ed.) (Notre Dame, IN: University of Notre Dame Press, 2003).

[53] See Davis; Ghoshal; Jensen; and MacIntyre.

[54] Charles Taylor, "The diversity of goods," in Stanley G. Clarke & Evan Simpson (eds.), *Anti Theory in Ethics and Moral Conservatism* (Albany, NY.: State University of New York Press, 1989), 223–240.

[55] MacIntyre.

[56] *Ibid.*

[57] Ghoshal.

[58] See Davis; and Ghoshal.

[59] David E. Garland, "The dispute over food sacrificed to idols (1 Cor. 8:1–11:1)," *Perspectives in Religious Studies* (30, 2003), 173–197. The arguments in the remainder of this paragraph are drawn from Garland.

[60] Garland.

[61] *Ibid.*

[62] *Ibid.*

[63] 1 Corinthians 8:4, NIV

[64] 1 Corinthians 10:23, NIV

[65] 1 Corinthians 10:23, NIV

[66] 1 Corinthians 9. Also Garland, 2003.

[67] See Garland.

[68] 1 Corinthians 10:1–22. Also Garland.

[69] 1 Corinthians 8:11–13 and 10:32–33

[70] 1 Corinthians 10:25–28

[71] Juho Hamari, Jonna Koivisto, & Harri Sarsa, "Does gamification work? – A literature review of empirical studies on gamification," *47th Hawaii International Conference on System Science* (Waikoloa, HI: IEEE. 2014), 3025–34.

[72] *Ibid.*

[73] See for example, Proverbs 20:23 and Ezekiel 22, respectively. Also, David Hagenbuch, "Honorable influence," *Christian Business Review* (5, 2017), 5–11.

[74] Nehemiah 5:1–5

[75] Leviticus 25

[76] Nehemiah 5:6–14

[77] Exodus 21:33–34

[78] Jeremiah 22:13; James 5:4

[79] Braverman.

[80] Federal Trade Commission, 2018. The Equifax data breach. https://www.ftc.gov/equifax-data-breach. Accessed June 4, 2018.

[81] Monsma.

[82] Mark Chaves, "SSSR Presidential Address: Rain dances in the dry season; Overcoming the religious congruence fallacy," *Journal for the Scientific Study of Religion* (2010), 1–14.

[83] Jason Stansbury, "Moral imagination as a reformational influence in the workplace," *Journal of Markets & Morality* (2015), 21–41.

[84] Patricia H. Werhane, *Moral Imagination and Management Decision-Making* (New York, NY.: Oxford University Press, 1999), also "Moral imagination and systems thinking," *Journal of Business Ethics* (38, 2002), 33-42, and "Mental models, moral imagination, and system thinking in the age of globalization," *Journal of Business Ethics* (78, 2008), 463–474.

[85] Werhane (1999).

[86] President John F. Kennedy, Remarks to an audience at the Free University of Berlin, collected in *One day in Berlin, 26 June 1963* (United States Government Agencies Collection, USG-02-B-1). Accessed June 7, 2018 at https://www.jfklibrary.org/AssetViewer/Archives/USG-02-B-1.aspx.

[87] Mavis Biss, Mavis, "Radical moral imagination: Courage, hope, and articulation," *Hypatia* (28(4), 2013), 937–954.

[88] Werhane (1999).

[89] David F. Caldwell & Dennis Moberg, "An exploratory investigation of the effect of ethical culture in activating moral imagination," *Journal of Business Ethics* (73, 2007), 193–204.

[90] Brian G. Whitaker & Lindsey N. Godwin, "The antecedents of moral imagination in the workplace: A social cognitive theory perspective," *Journal of Business Ethics* (114, 2013), 61–73.

[91] Denis G. Arnold & Laura P. Hartman, "Moral imagination and the future of sweatshops," *Business and Society Review* (108(4), 2003), 425-461. See also Timothy J. Hargrave, "Moral imagination, collective action, and the achievement of moral outcomes." *Business Ethics Quarterly* (19(1), 2009), 87–104.

[92] Caldwell & Moberg.

[93] Whitaker & Godwin.

[94] Arnold & Hartman.

[95] Hargrave.

[96] Colossians 2:8, NIV

[97] Immanuel Kant, *Critique of the Power of Judgment,* tr. Paul Guyer & Eric Matthews (Cambridge, UK: Cambridge University Press, 2009).

[98] Abraham Kuyper, *Wisdom & Wonder: Common Grace in Science & Art* (Grand Rapids, MI: Christian's Library Press, 2011).

[99] Wolters.

[100] Dyck (2013).

[101] Dyck (2013), 124–126.

[102] Werhane (2002) and (2008).

[103] James 2:14–26.

[104] Brueggemann.

[105] Werhane (2008).

[106] Romans 12:2, NIV

[107] Stansbury.

12

In Search of Abundance in an Age of Affluence: A Biblical Roadmap for Financial Priorities

By Ernest P. Liang

How We Erred on Stewardship

MUCH OF THE CONFUSION regarding stewardship within the Christian community suffers from what may be called a misguided role reversal. A steward, in the modern parlance, is an agent who is engaged by the principal (master, owner) to look after his/her affairs. The idea is for the agent to seek the best interest of the principal in return for the trust, and reward, of the engagement. In a role reversal, the agent usurps the identity of the principal and acts to best his own interest, taking a ride on the contractual relationship, wherein the owner becomes an impassive yet reliable provider of resources which the agent misconceives to be rightfully his own.

Believers acting on this misconception take seriously economic gains which they obtain by the sweat of their brow. They make financial decisions based on parameters that prioritize choices according to personal or familial desires while taking for granted the predictability of circumstances and the presumed boundless benevolence of the now owner-turned-agent Creator. To recast stewardship of financial matters in a proper framework requires resetting the parameters from a biblical perspective, righting the proper roles of agent vs. principal. This essay attempts to do that in the context of the decisions that define our everyday lives—how we spend, when we borrow, and what we must save.

To Buy or Not to Buy—The Stewardship of Consumption

"The world's largest economy grew faster in the third quarter than first estimated, capping its strongest six months in a decade, as *consumers went shopping...*" flashed the headline from *The Bloomberg News.*[1] For the US economy, it is hard to overemphasize the importance of consumer spending, which accounts for fully 70 percent of the national output. For the uninitiated and the pundit alike, consumption expenditure is a good recipe for arresting economic stagnation, if not a sure prescription for sustainable economic growth (and by implication, the standard of living).

While politicians and economists debate (and they have for a long time) about the role of demand (as in consumption) in lifting economic welfare, the conscientious Christ follower often struggles with the exact boundaries of indulgence and contentment when stewarding over consumption. Just as the author of Ecclesiastes declares, "So I commended pleasure, for there is nothing good for a man under the sun except to eat and to drink and to be merry, and this will stand by him in his toils throughout the days of his life which God has given him under the sun" (Eccl. 8:15 *NASB*), the apostle Paul would fondly remind us, "But godliness actually is a means of great gain when accompanied by contentment. For we have brought nothing into the world, so we cannot take anything out of it either. If we have food and covering, with these we shall be content" (1 Tim. 6:6-8).

A proper exegesis of these passages, however, presents principles that are in perfect harmony. Recognizing God as the ultimate source of our happiness, the celebration of life in response to His provision and goodness duly brings forth enjoyment out of a gratitude to God's loving kindness. A self-gratifying pursuit of material possessions and wonton pleasures is, therefore, a scorn to God's promise of joy from a life of divine priority and valuable commitments. For when we define significance in terms of luxury and abundance, we would have lost sight of His kingdom and His righteousness, from which all these other things, Lord willing, are to follow (Matthews 6:33).

The stewardship of consumption is, therefore, best discussed in the context of biblical priorities. These priorities establish a framework within which a spending plan, or budget, may be constructed according to individual circumstances. In a world awash in affluence (by historical standards and undoubtedly in America), much confusion arises in the discussion of needs and wants, necessities and luxuries, relaxation and indulgence, etc. The framework presented below abstracts from these discussions by offering a guideline for priorities in godly living. Starting with every dollar of disposable income, set aside portions that would meet these requirements (in the order presented). What is left for discretion beyond this list is, however, no less a testimony to one's faith and maturity in a purpose-driven life.

Giving

There is much written about giving in the Scriptures and in popular literature on Christian living. As Jim Elliott says, "He is no fool who gives what he cannot keep to gain what he cannot lose." Giving is simply rendering to God what belongs to Him as a testimony to our faithful stewardship of the resources entrusted to us. In setting priority for giving, two things stand out.

First, sacrificial giving is pleasing to God, as evidenced by Jesus' assessment of the widow's act of sacrifice (Mark 12:41-44). Second, giving is a means by which the materially blessed share in kind God's love and mercy to the less fortunate (thereby transforming corruptible earthly treasures into incorruptible heavenly treasures for themselves) (Matt. 19:21, Luke 16:7-9). As we contemplate giving, set a goal beyond what we ordinarily consider comfortable, and cheerfully add parachurch organizations serving the poor and needy to the recipient list. A faithful steward is held accountable for steering the entrusted resources to serve the master's best interests, and giving is but the proper administration of this duty.

Saving

From an economic standpoint, even the consumption advocates would have to admit that supply must precede demand, that in order to spend, we must first earn income by being gainfully employed. Savings, in the long run, constitute the source of funding for investment in business enterprises which offer the employment opportunities. At the personal level, savings meet the needs of contingencies and free us from societal/familial dependency after retirement. But perhaps the most important role of saving in the context of consumption is it enforces disciplined living. It is prudent to save a minimum of a quarter of the family's annual income just to meet retirement needs[2]. More should be set aside to provide for planned expenditures, such as children's college education and home or auto purchases. Something extra can be added to the pool to act as a restraint on self-indulging non-necessities and impulsive purchases. More guidelines about savings are discussed later in this essay.

Family Needs

The family (encompassing immediate and extended relatives) is the center of the covenant activity of God as portrayed in the Bible. Paul is quite unequivocal in inserting the family into our financial priority when he writes, "But if anyone does not provide for his own, and especially for those of his household, he has denied the faith and is worse than an unbeliever" (1 Tim. 5:8). There is, therefore, no excuse for us to ignore the *basic needs and comfort* of our immediate, and perhaps even extended, family when we set spending priorities. We also need to recognize that as stewards of the family God has entrusted to us, we please the master by ensuring our family's physical and spiritual well-being as well as by enabling the development of each member's God-given potential. Faith-enriching education and other development activities, such as Christian camps and mission trips, would fall into this category.

Personal Development Needs

Being a disciple literally means being a "learner." As wise stewards of the talents, gifts, and time God has given to us, we need to be studious life-learners so that we become the best worker we can be and the shrewdest manager of God's resources. Investing in learning through self-improvement and education (what economists called "human capital"), with a view to adding new skills (work related as well as social, emotional, and thinking) and useful knowledge, is perhaps the smartest deployment of available financial resources. After all, the "good and faithful servants" in Jesus' Parable of the Talents (Matthew 25:14-30) did not multiply their "talents" by sitting on their hands!

What Is Left

The Bible does not lay out the Christian walk by pounding on believers a load of "don'ts" except for what are clearly sinful desires and actions. As we expend God's resources, we should ponder on the guidelines in 1 Corinthians 10:23-24: "All things are lawful, but not all things are profitable. All things are lawful, but not all things edify. Let no one seek his own good, but that of his neighbor." If that lacks specificity for some, then Calvin's more direct advice may help: "While the liberty of the Christian in external matters is not to be tied down to a strict rule, it is, however, subject to this law—he must indulge as little as possible; on the other hand, it must be his constant aim not only to curb luxury, but to cut off all show of superfluous abundance, and carefully beware of converting a help into a hindrance."[3]

Till Debt Do We Part—The Stewardship of Borrowing

Graduating from college is meant to be an occasion to celebrate. Unfortunately for many graduates, it is also a somber reminder that it is time to pay back what they owe. According to the *Wall Street Journal*, the Class of 2014 was the most indebted class ever.[4] Over 70 percent of these graduates left school with student loans averaging a crushing $33,000. Student loans remain the fastest growing category (up over 360 percent since 2003) of US household debt. Total US household debt, on the other hand, grew 61 percent between 2003 and 2013.[5] According to one report, the average American is more than $225,000 in debt, with many having less than $500 in savings.[6]

In a society in which a certain perceived standard of living is regarded as a right of citizenship, and where the incentive to borrow is cemented by historic low interest rates and the prospect (even if illusory) of continued economic prosperity, the decision to go into debt often escapes serious scrutiny before the borrower signs on. To many, the question is not whether, but how much, to borrow, taking presumptions upon tomorrow which may or may not be realistic. The Christian may face the additional conundrum of whether indebtedness is biblical at all, but the fact that everybody (from individual believers to congregations) is doing it often dispels any remaining doubt.

It may be comforting for many Christians to know that the Scripture does not prohibit borrowing. It is clear from both Old and New Testament passages that the practice of lending/borrowing, even at interest (whether in currency or in kind), seems to be accepted business procedures (Deut. 23:19, 2 Kings 4:1-7, Matt. 25:27, Luke 16:7-9). But given the fact that the vast majority of debt in biblical times were incurred by the poor or needy to meet basic consumption needs, the proper context of loans in God's Word is more like an act of love. As a result, there is clear advice regarding the pledge of security (Deut. 24:6, Prov. 6:1), the need for release (Deut. 15:1-6), the evil of usury (Lev. 25:37), and the risk of enslavement (Prov. 22:7).

In today's modern economy, our needs have grown much beyond basic day-to-day consumption. For example, by deferring consumption, we can lend relatively safely for a positive rate of return and borrow (leverage) to invest in increased productivity, contributing to a higher standard of living for all. Savings to build a retirement nest egg and borrowing to earn an education illustrate the point. For the modern Christian facing a confusing array of needs and wants, what could be sensible instructions on borrowing based on the Scripture? The following guidelines (acronym "PASS"), which adhere to the general biblical principles of stewardship and a purpose driven life, may be proposed:

Profitability (P)

A borrower's ability to repay a loan with interest is undergirded by the accretive purpose of borrowed funds. The use of credit is to enhance, or leverage, the potential return on an investment. A loan purely for current consumption, such as a vacation or a new entertainment system, does not leverage, but one that augments future productivity, such as a college education or a new stamping machine for a machine shop does. Because credit card usages are primarily for services and ongoing consumption needs, to incur cumulative credit card debts requiring recurrent interest payments is not advisable. In contrast, our primary residence and private transportation means could be viewed partly as capital investments, as they do contribute to our ability to lead and grow a productive work-life. Home mortgages and auto loan for the family car can perhaps be justified to the extent that most people would find it difficult to acquire these assets with savings alone.

Affordability (A)

The primary obligation of the borrower is to repay the debt in full. According to Scripture, it is wickedness when one fails to do so: "The wicked borrows and does not pay back, but the righteous is gracious and gives" (Ps. 37:21). A prudent calculation on affordability will make sure a baseline discretionary cash flow (after budgeted giving, savings, and necessary expenditures but before debt service) is sufficient to service the debt until its maturity. If affordability is marginal, but the debt serves a good purpose, then the borrower should make sure there are enough assets that can be sold to repay the debt if necessary. Prudence in this context is to ensure plentiful margins so that one does not fall into insolvency.

Speculation's Folly (S)

It is paramount to consider the ability to repay a loan in unconditional terms, without making presumptions upon an uncertain future. The Book of James speaks to the folly of speculating about the future and the wisdom of a purpose driven life: "… you do not know what your life will be like tomorrow. You are just a vapor that appears for a little while and then vanishes away. ... you boast in your arrogance; all such boasting is evil. Therefore, to one who knows the right thing to do and does not do it, to him it is sin" (James 4:13-17). It is "arrogance" when people think they can somehow force square pegs into life's round holes or trust in their ability to restack life's circumstances to bring about favorable outcomes. If a loan requires picking up a second job or putting the spouse or a child to work, then it would be wise to first seek spiritual affirmation regarding whether the debt is consistent with God's purpose for our life. The same can be said about one's tendency to rely on the speculative future appreciation of assets to justify their acquisition of debt (example: flipping houses for profit during the 2008 financial crisis). We need to be reminded that a first principle of assuming debt, as laid out in the Pentateuch, is that such a transaction needs to be pleasing to both God and man. Despite the vast difference in economic circumstances between now and biblical times, the Godly wisdom about lending and borrowing never changes.

Stewardship (S)

Stewardship is all about serving our master for His best interest. With respect to resources entrusted to us by our heavenly Father, Jesus' Parable of the Talents (Matt. 25:14-30) is most revealing. The wicked servant was rebuked and punished for his laziness, for failing to earn a minimum, risk-free rate of return in bank interest. The faithful servants were praised and rewarded for their willingness to invest prudently and make a return over and above the opportunity cost of money (the bank's interest rate), which required discernment and some risk taking. How is this principle applied to the taking on of debt?

If we have discretionary resources that are generating a certain rate of return and a new investment opportunity arises, is it prudent to fund this new opportunity with debt instead of the existing resources? The simple answer is yes if the cost of borrowing is less than the rate of return earned on the existing investments. The more complete answer will depend on the riskiness of the new opportunity, the terms of the loan, and the predictability of the returns on the existing investments. However, it is reasonable to say that it is not always true to the statement "never borrow if you can afford not to." What is important is that we put God's entrusted resources to profitable use with wisdom, and all the guidelines discussed here, nicknamed "PASS," should be considered in their totality and not in isolation. Only in that way can we be wise users of debt.

The Crisis of Financial Insecurity— The Stewardship of Savings

According to a recent study by the Employee Benefit Research Institute, one-third of all American workers have a measly $1,000 saved for their retirement years. It says that 43 percent of Boomers and "Generation Xers" are at risk of running out of money in retirement. Among the poorest 25 percent, EBRI estimates a stunning 83 percent are at risk. Even more alarming, even these bleak numbers are based on the most optimistic financial scenarios![7]

This savings crisis happens against the backdrop of a stagnant average US household income, which, according to the US Census Bureau, has barely grown in real terms since the late 1990s. In a culture where the lure of material comfort, pleasure, and status is tantalizing, it is little wonder that excessive consumption reigns as the norm, resulting in historically low personal savings rates (of below 4 percent).

For Christians, it is clear the Scripture touts the virtue of savings. But it needs to be put into proper perspective. Since God is the rightful owner of all we have, our role is faithful steward and not hoarder of resources. Jesus' teaching in Matthew 6:19 ("Do not store up for yourselves treasures on earth") and the parable of the rich fool (Luke 12:15-21) make the point quite clear. To further the emphasis of trusting God in all circumstances, the apostle Paul was quick to point out that "if we have food and covering, with these we shall be content" (1 Tim. 6:8). Likewise, the writer of Hebrews reminds us: "Keep your lives free from the love of money and be content with what you have, because God has said, never will I leave you; never will I forsake you" (Heb. 13:5). What then, would be the objectives of savings given these scriptural teachings on contentment and trusting in God?

Savings Induce Disciplined Living

The overflowing abundance in our society often overwhelms our senses of living within our means, even if we sincerely desire so. In Proverbs 21:20 ("There is precious treasure and oil in the dwelling of the wise, but a foolish man swallows it up"), the contrast between the wise and the fool is not so telling in where they ended up as in how they got there—the act of squandering or devouring the resources entrusted to our care by God sets apart the foolish from the wise. Planned saving forces us to live responsibly. It is simply an act of wisdom in a materialistic world.

Savings Minimize Our Reliance on Debt

As a financial economist, I recognize the productive purposes of lending and borrowing in the modern economy. Even in personal finance, borrowing to acquire big-ticket assets (such as a home) that grow in value makes good economic sense as long as the debt service fits into a well-thought-out budget with planned savings. Savings, however, keeps us out of unwarranted indebtedness, which, after all, is enslaving and markedly inflates the total cost of a good or service (a form of "swallowing up" according to Proverbs 21:20). Saving is making provision for tomorrow, while debt is a presumption upon tomorrow. Habitual indebtedness is both a poor testimony and unfaithful stewardship. This is why Paul admonishes thus, "Let no debt remain outstanding..." (Rom. 13:8) and Proverbs 22:7 cautions, "The rich rules over the poor, and the borrower becomes the lender's slave."

Savings Answer to Times of Need

While life's uncertainties are enough reason for prudent saving practices, what Joseph did in Genesis 41 speaks to the necessity of careful planning for needs foreseen. Chief among these anticipated needs is the maintenance of a decent quality of life after we retire, when our income abilities diminish and our health inevitably deteriorates. Moreover, our withdrawal from the active workforce does not obviate our continued obligation to provide financially for our loved ones, which include not only our spouses but perhaps also our elderly parents and grown children should circumstances demand it. Paul is unequivocal in stressing the importance of a family safety net when he writes: "But if anyone does not provide for his own, and especially for those of his household, he has denied the faith and is worse than an unbeliever" (1 Tim. 5:8).

Savings Offer the Freedom for Ministry

Throughout Scripture the teaching on wealth has been remarkably consistent—it is a blessing in God's sovereignty toward those who are faithful and obedient, and it is a curse toward those who are "not rich toward God" (Luke 12:21). Therein lies the difference between saving and hoarding. Hoarding is wealth building for self-glorification, and saving is wealth building for fulfilling our witness to God's loving kindness. Not only is saving good stewardship because we can give to God's work (cf. 1 Cor. 16:2) but it is also our responsible answer to the Lord's command "not to worry about our lives" (Luke 12:22)—so that we can devote ourselves "worry free" to worthwhile ministries. While retirement is almost obligatory in modern secular work, it is not a known practice in the Scriptures. As we labor for the Kingdom in our advanced years, adequate savings would provide the freedom and means we need to be generous toward God.

Savings Bring a Legacy of Stewardship

Bequeathing an inheritance of material possessions is a virtue just as much as good character if it is built with integrity, discipline, and an eye toward nourishing our grandchildren to become good citizens of the Kingdom. Proverbs 13:22 appears to affirm this with the proclamation: "A good man leaves an inheritance to his children's children, and the wealth of the sinner is stored up for the righteous." The wisdom of this, however, is balanced on the understanding that the beneficiaries must be ready, wise stewards themselves. Proverbs 20:21 thus cautions: "An inheritance gained hurriedly at the beginning will not be blessed in the end." Andrew Carnegie was correct when he suggested that "the almighty dollar bequeathed to a child is an almighty curse." Even for the trained child, it would perhaps be prudent to leave enough to help fund worthwhile education and head starts on business. Anything in excess could easily be turned into a curse.

Larry Burkett said, "You can tell more about the spiritual lives of a couple by looking at their check book than by anything else."[8] Savings, planned with the express intent of giving for the glory of God, is a practice that enriches spiritual lives, a discipline of faithful stewardship. It is perhaps no coincidence, therefore, that both savings and salvation stem from the same root word.

Notes

*This article was originally published in the Fall 2015 "Focus on Stewardship" issue of the Center for Christianity in Business's *Christian Business Review.*

[1] Victoria Stilwell, "Spending by Households, Companies Propels U.S. Economy," *Bloomberg News*, Nov. 25, 2014, Accessed 2014, *www.bloomberg.com/news*.

[2] This is a rough rule of thumb based on a saver aiming to retire in 40 years with no loss from the current standard of living but leave a cashless estate. A low interest/inflation environment is also assumed. The required amount goes up considerably for an older worker and one who aims to build cash into the inheritance.

[3] John Calvin, *The Institutes of the Christian Religion* [1537], tr. Henry Beveridge, Online Library of Liberty, Chapter 10, Sec. 4, Accessed 2015, http://oll.libertyfund.org/titles/calvin-the-institutes-of-the-christian-religion?q=curb+luxury#Calvin_0038_1726.

[4] Phil Izzo, "Congratulations to Class 2014, Most Indebted Ever," *Wall Street Journal*, May 16, 2014, Accessed 2014, http://www.wsj.com.

[5] Neil Shah, "U.S. Household Debt Increases," *Wall Street Journal*, May 13, 2014, Accessed 2014, http://www.wsj.com.

[6] "In Today's Economy, Average American is 'Drowning' in More Than $225,000 of Debt," *www.gobankingrates.com*, September 10, 2013.

[7] Brett Arends, "Our Next Big Crisis will be a retirement crisis," March 3, 2014. Accessed 2014, http://www.marketwatch.com. See also Mandi Woodruff, "One Third of Americans only Have 1,000 Saved for Retirement," March 18, 2014, Accessed 2014, http://finance.yahoo.com/news.

[8] Larry Burkett, *The Complete Financial Guide for Young Couples* (David C. Cook, 1960), 19.

About the Authors

Randy Beavers is an Assistant Professor of Finance at Seattle Pacific University. His research interests include executive compensation and financial education. Before joining academia, he worked at the Bureau of Justice Statistics. He holds a PhD in finance from the University of Alabama.

Michael Cafferky has been a frequent contributor of peer-reviewed papers for CBFA Annual Conferences and publications since 2001. He is currently the editor of the *Journal of Biblical Integration in Business*. From 2003 to 2017, he served as professor in the school of business at Southern Adventist University. During his last three years there, he served as the endowed Ruth McKee Chair for Entrepreneurship and Business Ethics until his retirement in July 2017. Michael is the author of several academic publications, including two peer-reviewed university textbooks used by Christian colleges and universities: *Management: A Faith-based Perspective* (Pearson Education, 2012) and *Business Ethics in Biblical Perspective: A Comprehensive Introduction* (InterVarsity Press, 2015). He is also the co-author of the book *Breakeven Analysis: The Definitive Guide to Cost-Volume-Profit Analysis* (Business Expert Press, 2010, 2014). Michael has given presentations on the Scriptural foundations of business in the United States, Canada, Russia, Ghana, South Africa, Australia, Lebanon, Mexico, France, Rwanda, and the Philippines.

Denise Daniels is a Professor of Management at Seattle Pacific University. Her scholarly interests include the meaning of work, Sabbath, leadership, and motivation. Denise consults and provides executive coaching services in the areas of leadership development, workforce retention, and managing diversity. Denise earned her PhD from the University of Washington.

David W. Gill (www.ethixbiz.com; www.davidwgill.org) is an ethics writer, speaker, and consultant in Oakland, California. He is the author of seven books, including *It's About Excellence: Building Ethically Healthy Organizations* (Wipf & Stock, 2011). During a 40-year career, he served on the faculties of New College Berkeley, North Park University, St. Mary's College, and Gordon-Conwell Seminary.

Al Erisman is co-chair of the Theology of Work Project. Previously, he was Executive in Residence at Seattle Pacific University (17 years) and retired from Boeing after 32 years as Director of Research and Development for Computing and Mathematics. He has authored numerous books and articles and is editor and co-founder of *Ethix* magazine. Al holds a PhD in applied mathematics from Iowa State University.

Doris Gomez, originally from Austria, earned her MBA at the University of Economics & Business Administration in Vienna. After several years in the business world and years of experience in global trade, retail, manufacturing, and consulting, she completed her PhD in Organizational Leadership at Regent University's School of Business & Leadership. Upon completion of her PhD, she moved into the role of director for the MA in Organizational Leadership program. In October 2014, the Board of Trustees unanimously appointed her as dean of the School of Business & Leadership. She teaches in the school's master's and doctoral programs, serves on dissertation committees, and is also co-editor for *Inner Resources for Leaders*. Her research interests include leadership development in the online environment, online education and student retention, cross-cultural leadership issues, leadership formation, character formation in leaders, and the inner life of leaders.

Wallace Henley is senior associate pastor at Houston's Second Baptist Church and chair of the Belhaven University Master of Ministry Leadership Degree program. Wallace was a domestic policy aide in the Nixon White House and also worked in the US Department of Justice and House of Representatives. Author of more than 20 books—including the award-winning *Globequake: Living in the Unshakeable Kingdom While the World Falls Apart*—and co-author with Jonathan Sandys—great-grandson of Winston Churchill—of *God and Churchill: How the Great Leader's Sense of Divine Destiny Changed His Troubled World and Offers Hope for Ours*. He has conducted leadership conferences in 22 nations and was awarded an honorary doctorate by Encourager Seminary, New Delhi, India, for his leadership work. Wallace attended Samford University, Southwestern Seminary, and Trinity Theological Seminary and holds an MA in organizational management.

Buck Jacobs is the founder and a board member of The C12 Group (www.C12group.com), America's leading provider of Christian CEO/owner roundtable services. Prior to C12's founding in 1992, Buck served as board director and vice-president of sales of the S.H. Mack Company, a founding member of The Fellowship of Companies for Christ International (FCCI). Buck was instrumental in the global development of Mack, a successful Christ-centered business, which was later acquired by a large public company. Buck's earlier experiences include managing director of Sta-Power Italia, Spa., CEO of The Executive Development Institute, and president and director of R.G. Haskins/N.A. Strand Corp. Buck is the author of *A Light Shines Bright in Babylon – A Handbook for Christian Business Owners*, *A Strategic Plan for Ministry*, and *The Parable of The Janitor and the CEO*.

Don Lee is an Associate Professor of Management at Seattle Pacific University. His research interest includes strategic alliances, spiritual formation and work engagement, and innovation management. Before joining academia, Don worked at the Korean Institute for International Economic Policy and Nike Korea. He holds a PhD in strategic management from the University of Pittsburgh.

Ernest P. Liang is the director of the Center for Christianity in Business (CCB) and Associate Professor of Finance at the Archie W. Dunham College of Business, Houston Baptist University in Houston, Texas. Prior to his academic appointment, Dr. Liang studied finance and economics at the University of Chicago and spent close to three decades in the business world in consulting and executive roles. He is passionate about integrating faith and learning, and the promotion of lifelong learning for Christian business professionals—missions that undergird the work at CCB (www.hbu.edu/ccb).

Bill Mearse was chief operating officer for Accenture's Resources business and senior managing director of its Houston office until his retirement in November 2013. During his 33 years with Accenture, Bill served in several roles and worked with numerous clients on a global basis to deliver valued business outcomes. Since his retirement, Bill participates in private investments for entrepreneurial companies seeking high-growth opportunities and serves as a volunteer in various capacities at Baylor University, Houston Baptist University, and Baylor College of Medicine. Bill holds BBA (with honors) and MBA degrees from Baylor University.

About the Authors

Darren Shearer is the founder and CEO of High Bridge Books and Media, host of *Theology of Business Podcast* and HBU's *Christianity in Business Podcast,* creator of the *Biblical Standards for Businesses* course, and author of three books, including *The Marketplace Christian* and *Marketing Like Jesus.* A former captain in the US Air Force, Darren earned the United States Air Force Commendation Medal for his meritorious service in Kuwait during Operation Iraqi Freedom. Darren holds an MA in Practical Theology from Regent University (Virginia Beach, VA) and an Advanced Graduate Certificate in Management from Pace University (New York, NY). www.TheologyofBusiness.com

Jason M. Stansbury is the James and Judith Chambery Chair for the Study of Ethics in Business at Calvin College. He is the Executive Director of the Society for Business Ethics and has served on the Editorial Board for *Business Ethics Quarterly* since 2011. Jason's research interests include philosophical and social-scientific perspectives on virtue in organizations, theological and social-scientific perspectives on religious business ethics, accounting ethics, and organizational ethics programs. He earned his PhD in Organization Studies from Vanderbilt University.